Electric Blues

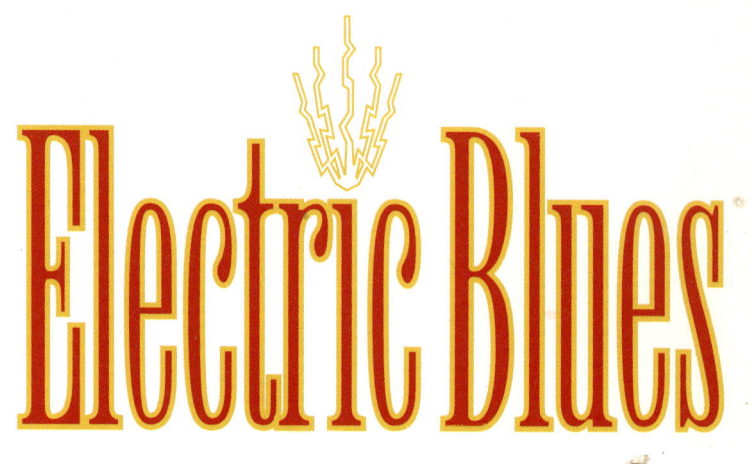

The Life, Times & Music® Series

Arthur "Big Boy" Crudup was among the first bluesmen to amplify his guitar, shortly after he began recording for Lester Melrose's Bluebird label in 1942. A talented composer, Crudup's "Mean Old Frisco" and "That's All Right" (a 1954 hit that helped launch the career of fellow Mississippian Elvis Presley) are among his better-known titles.

Electric Blues

The Life, Times & Music® Series

Erikka Haa

FRIEDMAN/FAIRFAX
PUBLISHERS

Acknowledgments

As always, special thanks to Nathaniel Marunas, for his continued guidance and support. I'd also like to thank the following individuals for their contributions to the production of *Electric Blues*: Doug Wygal, producer, Sony Music Special Products; Lori Thorne, designer, Elan Studio; Samantha Larrance, photo editor, Friedman/Fairfax; Tony Burgess and Mary Beth Curley, for sharing the gift of music with me (Hallmark would be proud); William Burr, Stan Williams, and Clarence Crawford, for their part in allowing me the necessary time off; the prodigious resources of the Performing Arts Library at Lincoln Center, the Donnell Library, and the Brooklyn Library; and the authors whose research and dedication to the history of the blues proved invaluable and whose efforts have helped keep the blues alive.

Dedication

To the men and women who have lived the blues.

"Blues, oh, Blues, you know you've been here before/
The last time you were here you made me cry and walk the floor."
—Ida Cox, from "Rambling Blues" (1925)

A FRIEDMAN/FAIRFAX BOOK

© 1996 by Friedman/Fairfax Publishers

All rights reserved. No part of this publication may be reproduced, stored in a retrieval system, or transmitted, in any form or by any means, electronic, mechanical, photocopying, recording, or otherwise, without prior written permission from the publisher.

ISBN 1-56799-298-6

Editor: Nathaniel Marunas
Art Director: Jeff Batzli
Design: Elan Studio
Photography Editor: Samantha Larrance
Production Manager: Jeanne E. Kaufman

Grateful acknowledgment is given to authors, publishers, and photographers for permission to reprint material. Every effort has been made to determine copyright owners of photographs and illustrations. In the case of any omissions, the publishers will be pleased to make suitable acknowledgments in future editions.

Color separations by HK Scanner Arts Int'l Ltd.
Printed in Hong Kong and bound in China by Midas Printing Limited

For bulk purchases and special sales, please contact:
Friedman/Fairfax Publishers
Attention: Sales Department
15 West 26th Street
New York, NY 10010
(212) 685-6610 FAX (212) 685-1307
Website: http://www.webcom.com/friedman/

Contents

Introduction 6

Backwater Blues 9

Texas Blues 18

Memphis Blues 23

Sweet Home Chicago 33

The West Side 43

Standin' at the Crossroads 53

The British Invasion 57

Epilogue 60

Suggested Reading 62

Suggested Listening 62

Index 63

Introduction

Africans, whose gods were never suppressed, didn't have the blues—they had no reason to have them. But a people deprived of religion, language, customs and human dignity did. The first slaves were the first bluespeople: America, literally, gave the slaves the blues.

—Julio Finn

Music has been an integral part of the African cultural tradition for centuries. Author and bluesman Julio Finn cites Barbadian reggae artist Dennis Bovell, who holds that "In the beginning there was the Sound." This contrasts with Christianity's claim that civilization began with "the Word," a mode of communication only human beings possess. Author Eileen Southern notes that early travelers to the "dark continent" rarely failed to comment on the importance of music and dance in the lives of the African people. For instance, English sea captain Richard Jobson, upon his return from exploring trade routes along the Gambia River in West Africa in 1620, wrote, "There is without doubt, no people on the earth more naturally affected to the sound of musicke than these people...."

This Currier and Ives painting shows slave life on a Mississippi plantation. This life of servitude was the primary fuel that propelled countless African Americans to flee to the North beginning in the nineteenth century.

Introduction

King Cotton mercilessly ruled over the lives of African Americans for centuries and is a commonplace theme in the blues. In 1929 author Rupert B. Vance described the Delta region as "cotton obsessed, Negro obsessed, and flood ridden, it is the deepest South, the heart of Dixie, America's super-plantation belt."

One of the most important functions of this cultural tradition is communication, music being the principal means of imparting news—of births, deaths, and nearly every other event in the life of the African. Traveling African musicians, or griots, were often described as living libraries; the griots preserved tribal stories and legal codes and were considered guardians of the people's folklore and history. Some griots were also known to be practitioners of voodoo, but as author Francis Bebey contends, "the role of the griot in West African society extends far beyond the realm of magic. The fact that music is at the heart of all the griot's activities is yet further proof of the vital part he plays in African life." The American bluespeople carry on the African griot's legacy.

The first West Africans arrived in Jamestown, Virginia, in 1619 as indentured servants, bringing their cultural heritage with them. Despite the fact that they were eventually entirely stripped of their freedom and bound to a lifetime of slavery, the traditions of these early Americans continued to evolve, adapting to life in an essentially hostile and foreign land. The slaves lost everything except their religion, which itself was branded "superstition," and were forced underground by their captors, who believed that Africans were a barbaric people incapable of culture.

Accordingly, slaves were not formally educated. Efforts to convert the slaves to Christianity were vigorous, however: the slave masters sought thereby to break

Introduction

An influential figure in the history of the "Great Awakening," a religious movement of the 1730s that called for (among other things) livelier music in church services, English minister Dr. Isaac Watts had published his Hymns and Spiritual Songs *(1707), which was very popular among African American slaves in the colonies.*

the bond between the newly arrived Africans and their homeland. The white God promised salvation for the soul of the black man in exchange for his body, which was sold into unimaginable suffering for the duration of his earthly existence. If the oppressor could gain control of the spirit of the oppressed, the potential for exploitation would increase while the likelihood of rebellion would vastly diminish.

The stolen children of Africa did not abandon their gods, but they did find it necessary to keep their tribal rites a secret from the slave master. And so the slave came to lead a double life, pandering to his captor's belief in his inherent lack of humanity while continuing to observe his cultural traditions and keeping hope alive through ritual and music. The first African Americans used the only means they had at their disposal, channeling their creativity into their music, which resulted in the parallel development of spirituals and the blues.

The songs of slaves, in keeping with the African tradition of music as a means of communication, were often used to impart information about secret camp meetings or rebellions. These songs were commonly disguised within a Christian context. For example, "The Gospel Train" was a spiritual that indirectly referred to Harriet Tubman's (c.1820–1913) Underground Railroad; upon hearing the song a slave could be sure that a "conductor" was on the way.

The missionary Dr. Isaac Watts (1674–1748) provided the basis for many of these songs through the hymns he taught to slaves. To many of the slaves Watts reached, however, "Canaan" and "Heaven" became metaphors for escape—at first back to Africa, and later to the North. These songs became the African American spirituals of the nineteenth century, which later transformed into what is now known as gospel.

Slaves toiling in the cotton fields or in chain gangs also sang songs, to ease the burden of their hardship and provide a rhythm for their labor. Developing alongside spirituals (in particular those spirituals known as sorrow songs), these work songs and field hollers in turn became the basis for the blues that rose out of the Mississippi Delta around the turn of the century. Unlike gospel, which encompassed such issues as relief from corporal torment in a merciful afterlife, the blues dealt with the daily burdens and joys of the here and now (harking back to the traditions of West Africa).

By the time of the Emancipation Proclamation of 1863, a new and entirely American form of music had taken shape. Gerard Herzhaft aptly described the cornerstone of this distinctly American music: "Above all, the Delta blues is characterized by its powerful bass notes and an insistent rhythm that came directly from its African origins."

Backwater Blues

They wanted the sun to go down so they could stop working, they worked so hard. They learned the blues from that.
—Shelby Brown to William Ferris, Leland, Mississippi, 1974

The fertile Delta area, considered by many musicologists to be the birthplace of the blues, extends northward from Memphis, Tennessee, with Vicksburg, Mississippi, to the east and the Mississippi River to the west. The area remained mostly undeveloped until the 1820s, but by 1835 had become an extension of the cotton empire. Slavery took a different form during the post–Civil War period as plantations began using African American labor under the sharecropper system.

Despite the promise of freedom in the Emancipation Proclamation, African Americans were still exploited and oppressed following the Civil War. Indeed, many ex-slaves continued to work on the same plantations they had worked on before, this time under a system that kept them in debt to their "former" masters. The first enactment of "Jim Crow" legislation in the South, in 1890, enforced

The life of the "roustabout" or "stevedore" (pictured above in St. Louis in the 1890s) on the banks of the Mississippi River or aboard the steamships that navigated the black waters of the mighty waterway was a harsh one—mules were valued above men, and women were worked as hard as either. The docks along the river's waterfront were rife with murder and corruption; the docks were also subject to natural disasters, including the 1927 flood that quickly overwhelmed the levees and left over 750,000 people homeless.

Backwater Blues

Conditions in the Jim Crow South underlined the country's continued subscription to ignorance and racism, as this 1939 photo of "separate but equal" drinking fountains in Oklahoma City depicts. The system of laws, named after a caricature common to minstrel shows, remained in effect from the 1880s until the legislation was appealed after the mid-1950s.

"separate but equal" segregation of African Americans—in case there was any doubt as to their citizenship status. Considering the harsh conditions of the Reconstruction Era South, it is hardly surprising that many of the region's disenfranchised citizens simply left. This accounted for the first large-scale migration of ex-slaves to northern urban areas, in 1865.

During the massive African American migrations following the Civil War, World War I, and World War II, many Delta bluesmen traveled to the larger urban cities of Chicago or Detroit in search of better opportunities. The noisy clubs and back alleys of the northern ghettos proved a challenge to musicians accustomed to performing at plantation shacks, dance halls, and backyard fish-fries in a peaceful countryside.

The advent in the 1930s of the electric guitar, the first popularly manufactured electric instrument, changed the face of popular music in the United States. Electric blues increased the volume of the bluesman's sound, helping him to overcome the din of urban life.

As we have seen, the blues were born when the first Africans set foot on North American shores more than four hundred years ago. And although the slaves certainly influenced early American music through work songs and spirituals, and had even entertained their masters in plantation parlors throughout the South, African American musicians were not formally recognized as such until well after Emancipation.

Among the earliest of the "professional" blues singers, Gertrude "Ma" Rainey (1886–1939) remembered first hearing the blues in 1902, according to author Eileen Southern. Rainey was touring in Missouri with the Rabbit Foot Minstrels when she heard a local girl sing a song about the man who had deserted her. Soon, Rainey and

The Guitar

According to Gerard Herzhaft, the guitar was first introduced in the United States by Mexican *vaqueros* working in Texas. It became popular and affordable around the same time that the first bluesmen were being recorded, thereby coinciding with the spread of blues. In addition, the guitar's flexibility allowed for the production of "blue" notes, the alterations in scale characteristic of the blues.

The distinct sound of the bottleneck or slide guitar was originally produced using a sawed-off glass bottleneck (later replaced with a metal tube), usually worn on the little finger of the left hand and slid along the top of the strings. Possibly Hawaiian in origin, the technique magnifies the effect of "blue notes" and has become particularly characteristic of American blues. The Hawaiian style of guitar playing is noted for the guitar being held on the lap, although few bluesmen employ this method.

The advent of the guitar solo is most often attributed to Lonnie Johnson, although Sylvester Weaver (1897–1960) was the first male ever to record the blues guitar, with his "Guitar Blues" and "Guitar Rag" in October 1923. Johnson, however, developed the style of blues called "flatpicking," where the melody is played note by note with the use of a pick. Blues legend Robert Johnson adopted the jazz guitarist's last name and claimed they were brothers with the hope of capitalizing on Lonnie Johnson's fame.

In fact, many current electric guitar styles—from modern to blues to jazz to rock—can ultimately be traced to the genius of Lonnie Johnson, who influenced early jazz electric guitar players Charlie Christian and Floyd Smith, as well as early electric blues guitar players like T-Bone Walker.

Gibson started the electric guitar revolution in 1936. Trombonist/guitarist Eddie Durham, from Count Basie's band, had attempted to amplify the guitar for years before Gibson's breakthrough. Durham is credited with alerting master jazzman Charlie Christian to the electric model by 1937. Christian immediately understood that the electrification of the guitar would enable it to compete as a solo instrument with the saxophone.

In 1948 another revolution began when Fender Musical Instruments of California began work on the first commercially successful solid-body guitar, the Telecaster. The added sustain and resistance to feedback, which had plagued the hollow instruments, helped popularize the electric guitar even further as a solo voice. In conjunction with the relatively high-wattage Fender amplifiers, one or two guitars working together could produce a sound big enough to take the place of an entire horn section, making small combos the perfect choice for the pervasive club scene. By the 1950s, big-band ballroom music was on the wane as bars, lounges, and roadhouses were rocking to the exuberance and power of electric blues.

Above: A graceful and agile performer, Texas legend T-Bone Walker, pictured here in 1968 in a pose reminiscent of the Hawaiian style of guitar playing, was among the first bluesmen to play electric guitar in 1936 and influenced many subsequent blues and rock guitarists, from B.B. King to Jimi Hendrix. Below: The legendary Fender Telecaster.

her vaudeville group were incorporating a popular ensemble-based style of the blues in their shows. With the publication of W.C. Handy's (1873–1958) "Memphis Blues" and "St. Louis Blues," the genre had gained fairly widespread exposure. Movers and shakers in the budding recording industry began to sit up and take notice.

Beginning with the release of Mamie Smith's (1883–1940) "Crazy Blues," recorded in New York in 1920 and considered by many to be the first commercial blues record, major record companies—which were all controlled by white entrepreneurs—profited in an expanding "race music" market by recording black artists to promote to black record buyers. The blues, which mirrored the laments and triumphs of its listeners, had a ready market in African American communities across the nation.

The radio became an important means of exposure for "race records" throughout the South and in the larger cities of the North as radio stations be-

Mamie Smith—among the first African American blues singers to be recorded commercially—scored a huge success in 1920 with her recording of "Crazy Blues" (OKeh sold seventy-five thousand copies during the first month of the song's release). From her early popularity in Harlem in 1914 until 1931, by which time she had recorded about one hundred sides, Smith was one of the most in-demand blues artists in the world. Typical of the times, however, she died in poverty and obscurity in New York City on October 30, 1940.

The success of King Biscuit Time *on radio station KFFA in Helena, Arkansas, inspired other stations in the area to follow suit, including KWEM in West Memphis and WDIA in Memphis. Pictured from left to right (in addition to the announcer, Mr. Langston) are King Biscuit Boys Joe "Willie" Wilkins, Robert "Dudlow" Taylor, Sonny Boy Williamson (Rice Miller), James "Peck" Curtis, and Willie Love.*

gan broadcasting programs specifically aimed at a black audience. From several hours to as many as twenty-four hours a day listeners could tune in to continuous programs of blues and gospel, both live and prerecorded. One of the best-known and longest-lived of these programs came from station KFFA in Helena, Arkansas. In 1941 the country-blues program called *King Biscuit Time* began broadcasting live and continued without interruption until 1981.

"Rice" (Sonny Boy Williamson #2) Miller (c. 1899–1965) and the stepson of Robert Johnson (1911–1938), guitarist Robert "Junior" Lockwood (b. 1915) inaugurated the program in November 1941 and within a year had added Willie Wilkins (guitar), Dudlow Taylor (piano), and Peck Curtis (drums). The show advertised King Biscuit Flour and, in homage to Miller, Sonny Boy Corn Meal. Because Helena's central location in the Mississippi Delta region ensured a large listening audience, for a period of time the show was broadcast simultaneously from Clarksdale, Mississippi, on station WROX, reaching through Arkansas and into the Delta with a range of more than one hundred miles (160km).

Following Sonny Boy's lead, many of the important post–World War II bluesmen appeared on *King Biscuit Time* or on similar shows on KFFA over the years, among them James "Peck" Curtis (1912–1970), David "Honeyboy" Edwards (b. 1915), "Little" Walter Jacobs (1930–1968), Willie Love (1911–1957), Muddy Waters, Robert Nighthawk (1909–1967), Jimmy Rogers, Houston Stackhouse (1910–1980), Joe "Willie" Wilkins (1923–1979), and Elmore James.

Elmore James (1918–1963)

Had Robert Johnson lived to play electric guitar, he may well have sounded like slide meister Elmore James. As the spiritual and musical heir to the King of the Delta Blues, James became the inspiration for every slide guitarist who has heard his bone-rattling blues.

—Dave Rubin

Little is known about the early days of Elmore James, born Elmore Brooks to fifteen-year-old Leola Brooks and (probably) Joe Willie "Frost" James on January 27, 1918, in Richland, Mississippi. It seems he spent a lot of time on the road as a young boy, his

Heavily inspired by the enigmatic Robert Johnson (whose "Dust My Broom" became James' biggest hit in 1952), Elmore James, performing for over three decades despite poor health, became one of the most influential bluesmen of all time, both in the United States and abroad.

Elmore James, reticent and shy offstage, utilized a powerful singing style and slashing guitar technique that became the inspiration for nearly every slide guitarist to come after him, from J.B. Hutto to John Mayall.

parents finding work where they could on the various plantations along Highway 51 in Holmes County, Mississippi. A distant cousin remembers James playing a cheap guitar and singing "Dust My Broom" and "Smokestack Lightning" for Saturday night dances in the small community of Franklin.

James' family moved to Belzoni, in the heart of the Delta, in 1937 in a mostly vain attempt to eke out a better living as sharecroppers. On the Kincaid plantation they adopted an orphan, Robert Earl Hosten, who shared James' interest in playing the blues. With Hosten on rhythm guitar and James on lead, the twosome played on the plantation and in the jukes of Belzoni when they could find work.

James was nineteen by then and developing a taste for the rambling life of the Delta bluesman. Music became the most important thing in his life and he decided to leave the farm behind. He took Josephine Harris, a local girl, as his bride, bought a twenty-dollar guitar, and hit the road. Along the way he met up with Robert "Junior" Lockwood and Sonny Boy Williamson #2; the latter would become a constant companion, but it was Robert Johnson who inspired James to use a slide.

Johnson died in Greenwood on August 16, 1938, by which time Sonny Boy and James had become very close. By 1939 James was working on the Daybreak plantation and Sonny Boy would often come to Belzoni to play with and see his friend James, who had put together a small band (despite the fact that he preferred to play alone) with his adopted brother. With Precious White (sax), Tutney Moore (trumpet), and Frock O'Dell (drums), they played dances at places like the Harlem Theater in Hollandale, the Midnight Grill in Tchula, the Peacock Inn in Belzoni, and Big Boy Cray's juke joint near Goodman.

James was drafted into the navy in July 1943, returning to Belzoni in November 1945 after active duty in Guam and an honorable discharge. He found his parents had divorced and moved to Chicago, while his brother had stayed behind to start a radio business in Canton, where James stayed for a year. It was around this time that his heart condition was detected and James, only twenty-eight years old, had to be hospitalized in Jackson.

Originally recorded by Robert Johnson in 1936, later covered by "Big Boy" Crudup in 1949 and Robert "Junior" Lockwood in 1951, and one of the best-known pieces in blues history, "Dust My Broom" was solidified as a blues classic by Elmore James.

James had resumed his friendship with Sonny Boy on frequent trips to Helena and by 1947 was back in Belzoni working on the Silver Creek plantation, trying to pick up the pieces of his marriage and his musical career. Sonny Boy lent a helping hand by coming down to Belzoni and including James on a radio show advertising Talaho, a patent medicine, for the O.J. Turner Drug Store. The program, broadcast from radio station WAZF in Yazoo City or WJPJ in Greenville, was a great success and led to a better offer for Sonny Boy from another patent medicine, Hadacol, which advertised over KWEM in West Memphis, where Sonny Boy moved in 1949.

Although he enjoyed recording with Sonny Boy, James, perhaps because of his inherent and at times debilitating shyness, was reluctant to release a record of his own. Lillian McMurphy of Trumpet Records took matters into her own hands by recording James without his knowledge during a rehearsal session for "Dust My Broom." James was very upset by the maneuver, and despite the fact that the record entered the R&B charts on April 5, 1952, and eventually reached the top ten, he adamantly refused to cut a follow-up and never recorded for Trumpet again.

The offers began to pour in from Chess and others, until Joe Bihari of Modern Records finally persuaded James to move up to Chicago to record. While staying with his uncle Mac Willie James at 4714 S. Evans, James played his first club date with Kansas City Red at Chuck's (on Damen and Madison on the South Side) and recorded with Johnnie Jones' (c. 1924–?) band for the Bihari brothers' subsidiary Meteor in late autumn of 1952. Other recording sessions followed, including one for Chess subsidiary Checker on January 17, 1953, although the recordings were never released, probably because of James' contract with the Biharis. In November of the same year, again with Jones' band, he recorded some outstanding sides for the Flair label, including "Hawaiian Boogie" and "Make a Little Love."

"Homesick" James (b. 1910) remembered the sessions with Elmore and Jones' band fondly, recalling for author Mike Rowe how "Elmore and Johnnie used to just have a fight every night. That was the whole point....After they get to, y'know, yakkin' each other then the band would get lively. Everybody be in there—whole big party, yessir!"

Despite a brief stint with the Maxwell Davis band in Hollywood, Elmore's record sales were slipping, leading the Biharis to drop him in 1955; his last release was the appropriately titled "Goodbye Baby" for the subsidiary Flair label. Down but far from out, James continued to play regularly the following year at West Side clubs like Sylvio's, the Key Largo, Charlie's Lounge, and Club Alex.

The dry spell broke in 1957 when James, just out of the hospital after his second heart attack, was offered a recording contract by Mel London of the Chief label. Homesick James and Eddie Taylor (1923–1985) played second and rhythm guitar, respectively (all three were plugged into the same amplifier), for the first session, which produced some very exciting sides including "Coming Home." But aside from a reissue by VeeJay not long afterward and although other sessions did follow, James' comeback to the recording scene was impressive but brief.

After a brief stint in 1958 as a deejay on WRBC in Jackson—and despite his failing health—James returned to Chicago's clubs, where he was still very popular. There he was tracked down by producer Bobby Robinson, of Fire Records in New York, who had admired James since first hearing "I Believe"; recording sessions were arranged. The classic blues "The Sky Is Crying," recorded for Fire in November 1959, has witnessed many versions since, notably James' own re-recording for Chess in April 1960. Subsequent releases include those by Freddie King, Albert King, Sonny Boy Williamson #2, and Stevie Ray Vaughan (1954–1990).

In 1962 James retreated to Jackson after being blacklisted from Chicago for nonpayment of his 1961 union dues (the first black musician's union, Chicago's Local 208, was incorporated into the American Federation of Musicians in 1902). While in Jackson he continued to record for Fire Records; there were also sessions with harp player Sam Myers in New Orleans. Later, disc jockey and record promoter Big Bill Hill had straightened out James' problems with the union in Chicago and in May 1963 sent for him to play at Hill's new Copa Cobana Club.

James was staying with his cousin Homesick and his wife while playing at the Copa on Monday and Tuesday nights. On Wednesday, May 22, 1963, James went to Union Hall to renew his contract; by the evening of Friday, May 24, Elmore James, one of the best-loved bluesmen of his time, was dead (attributed to heart failure). Released by Bobby Robinson just a few months after James' death, the aptly titled "It Hurts Me Too" was a great success.

Texas Blues

The blues come to Texas/Loping like a mule....
— Blind Lemon Jefferson, from *Got the Blues*

In addition to the state itself, the area falling under the influence of the Texas style of blues includes parts of Louisiana, Oklahoma, and New Mexico, and extends along the Santa Fe Railroad into California (the West symbolizing for Texas what the North did for the Delta). From the pine woods of the northeast to the rolling plains of western Texas, the Lone Star state encompasses a vast region and consequently a rich variety of influences. The Cajun influence of southern Louisiana left its mark on the area around Beaumont in the southeast; Dallas, with its fertile cotton fields, was strongly influenced by the Delta blues, as were the fertile farmlands of Houston.

From the cultural heritage of this particular region came a blues with a distinct Spanish style, adopting flamenco phrasing into its melody. Among the progenitors of Texas blues in the 1920s were Lonnie Johnson (1894–1970), Leadbelly (1885–1949), and Blind Lemon Jefferson (1897–1930), an early influence on T-Bone Walker.

Railroad stations were a favorite hangout of rambling bluesmen during the periods of intense African American migration, and the blues is rife with images of going "down the line." The Illinois Central carried many a Delta bluesman to Chicago, where the blues became electrified, but you had to ride the Rock Island Line if you wanted to find the home of the man whom many have called the "Father of Electric Blues": T-Bone Walker.

T-Bone Walker (1910–1975)

Man, I didn't start playing the blues ever....That was in me before I was born, and I've been playing and living the blues ever since.
—T-Bone Walker

Together with Charlie Christian (1916–1942) and Eddie Durham (1906–1987), T-Bone Walker was among the first to pick up the new electric Spanish guitar shortly after it was introduced by Gibson in 1936. Generally credited as the first blues guitarist to play electric (he released "I Got a Break Baby" and "Mean Old World" in July 1942), Walker was a showman and pioneer in the development of the electric guitar sound, influencing the playing styles of Jimi Hendrix (1942–1970), Albert King, Buddy Guy, Otis Rush, Eric Clapton (b. 1945), Stevie Ray Vaughan, Clarence "Gatemouth" Brown, and Freddie King, to name a few.

Born Aaron Thibeaux Walker on May 28, 1910, in Linden, Texas, T-Bone's family moved to Dallas when he was two. While living in Dallas, the young Walker befriended and was inspired to play the guitar by Blind Lemon Jefferson, a friend of the family. No doubt due in large part to an early association with electric jazz guitar innovator Charlie Christian, Walker was also heavily influenced by that cousin of the blues from New Orleans. This would account for the strains of Louis Jordan (1908–1975) evident in the Texas guitar shuffle that Walker popularized, which in turn influenced the playing styles of Albert Collins and "Guitar" Slim (1926–1959).

By the mid-1920s Walker was accomplished enough on the guitar to join the Dr. Breeding Medicine Show, as well as participate in various carnivals held throughout the Lone Star state. Aside from his talent as a guitar player, he was also a tap dancer and performed in local vaudeville shows, notably sharing the stage with Ida Cox (1889–1967), the "Queen Without a Crown" of the blues.

In 1929 Walker recorded "Wichita Falls Blues" and "Trinity River Blues" for Columbia Records. Two blues in the Texas tradition, they were played on acoustic guitar under the name Oak Cliff T-Bone (Oak Cliff was an area of Dallas where he lived, beginning around 1920). The following year he played banjo in Cab Calloway's band as a result of winning a Dallas talent contest.

Walker moved to Los Angeles in the late 1930s and by 1940 was a featured performer in the Les Hite Orchestra. One of the first bluesmen to amplify his guitar, Walker set the trend for things to come. Recording sessions with Freddie Slack's band for Capitol Records ensued, and in 1942 the "T-Bone Shuffle" became a blues anthem.

Walker's "Call It Stormy Monday," recorded in Hollywood for Capitol Records in mid-1947 with Teddy Buckner (trumpet), Bump Meyers (tenor sax), Arthur Edwards (bass), Lloyd Glenn (piano), and Oscar Lee Bradley (drums), influenced many aspiring blues guitarists. John Lee Hooker received his first guitar from

Opposite: T-Bone Walker (pictured here in the 1940s) came from a long line of influential Texas bluesmen including Huddie Ledbetter (Leadbelly), Blind Lemon Jefferson, Alger "Texas" Alexander, Lightnin' Hopkins, and Lowell Fulson. In terms of stage presence and showmanship, however, Walker stood alone.

Freddie King (1934-1976)

Once asked if he, B.B. King, and Albert King were brothers, Freddie King responded with "We're brothers. We just don't have the same mother." Freddie King, who grew up listening to Louis Jordan and was influenced by the likes of T-Bone Walker and B.B. King, was born to Ella Mae Christian in Gilmer, Texas, on September 3, 1934. He saved enough money from picking cotton to buy his first guitar, a Roy Rogers model, by the time he was six. Early on King developed a sound similar to that of T-Bone Walker—whose guitar sound many described as hornlike—by trying to imitate Jordan's horn with his guitar while listening to the jazz saxophonist on a radio program called *In the Groove*.

With the common post–World War II hope of improving their lot, King's family moved to Chicago during the winter of 1949–1950. Big for his age at sixteen, King went to work for a steel mill almost immediately, but harbored hopes of breaking into the music scene of a city that was fast becoming a blues mecca. By the next year he had saved up enough money to buy himself an electric guitar.

Hanging around the Chicago blues scene as best as could be expected of someone his age, King gradually drew the attention of some of the city's established bluesmen, including that of the crowned "King of Chicago Blues" himself. As King recalled in a 1973 television interview, Muddy Waters used to sneak him in the back way at the Club Zanzibar on 13th and Ashland on Chicago's West Side. After a gig King usually went straight home and tried to imitate what he had witnessed performed onstage. He also received tutoring from Water's second guitarist, Jimmy Rogers, in addition to Eddie Taylor and Robert "Junior" Lockwood.

King met guitarist Jimmy Lee Robinson (b. 1931), who was fresh out of prison, in 1952. King had lined up a club date and was trying to get a band together in a hurry. Things did not look good at first—Robinson's guitar was in pawn and they didn't even have an amplifier—but King was optimistic. Somehow they managed; after getting the guitar out of pawn, borrowing another, and sharing an amplifier, they pulled off the show.

With the addition of drummer Sonny Scott, they became the Every Hour Blues Boys and began playing such clubs as Cadillac Baby's for about a year before both King and Robinson joined harp player Little Sonny Cooper's band. Later they went their separate ways, Robinson joining Elmore James and King going on to a successful solo career.

After a brief stint with John Burton's El-Bee label, King came to the attention of King Records, which pacted him to its subsidiary, Federal, in 1960. "Hide Away" was recorded on August 26 of that year for King Records in Cincinnati with Gene Redd, Clifford Scott (reeds), Bill Willis (bass guitar), Sonny Thompson (piano), and Philip Paul (drums). One of Freddie King's most successful recordings, the instrumental "Hide Away" had been an opening number for Hound Dog Taylor for several years before King recorded it for the Federal label.

During his "second coming" in the 1970s, King revived two of Jimmy Rogers' hits from the 1950s, "Walking By Myself" and "That's All Right," performing them on acoustic guitar for his Shelter label debut, *Getting Ready*. When it appeared that Shelter was open to other blues performers, King suggested recording his old mentor and in 1972 coproduced and played on one of the sessions for Rogers' *Gold Tailed Bird*.

Freddie King's last performance was on Christmas Day, 1976, at the New York Ballroom in Dallas. He died three days later of acute pancreatitis at the age of forty-two.

Singer, songwriter, and rockin' guitarist Freddie King, also known as the "Texas Cannonball," crossed the line from blues to soul to rock, equally at home playing beside Atlantic Records' King Curtis or rock legend Leon Russell.

A versatile and accomplished guitarist who could play more than just the blues, T-Bone Walker moved to California in 1934 and worked with Freddie Slack and Les Hite before getting his own band together. Pictured here on tour with the Les Hite Orchestra (a swing band) in the 1940s, Walker takes the mike at the Apollo Theater in Harlem, New York City.

Walker, and as B.B. King was quoted in *Guitar Player* magazine, "When I heard T-Bone Walker play the electric guitar, I just had to have one."

At the peak of his career, Walker hit the road on all-star "Battle of the Blues" tours, sharing star billing with such artists as Ray Charles (b. 1930), Lowell Fulson (b. 1921), Wynonie Harris (1915–1969), Big Joe Turner (1911–1985), and Jimmy Witherspoon (b. 1923). Because Walker's energetic performance was such a hard act to follow, he inevitably was the closing act at all the shows.

Booking agent Harold Oxley helped Walker land bigger and more lucrative gigs; backed by Jim Wynn's band, the guitarist toured extensively from the late 1940s until 1955. He signed with Imperial Records in 1950, recording over fifty songs with that label alone, which helped him maintain his career over the next four years. In addition Walker cut numerous sides for Capitol, Black & White, and such smaller, independent labels as Rhumboogie and Old Swingmaster.

Walker took part in the first European tour of the American Folk Blues Festival in 1962; he would return to Europe several times from 1962 to 1974, following the initial warm reception he had enjoyed from the many jazz and blues fans overseas. Although his early influences were country blues, Walker's was a more sophisticated swing and jazz-tinged blues style, in the tradition of Lonnie Johnson and Eddie Lang. In 1966 he recorded an album in the *Jazz at the Philharmonic* series featuring Duke Ellington and Oscar Peterson, and the following year he appeared at the Monterey Jazz Festival.

T-Bone Walker suffered a stroke on New Year's Eve, 1974, and was admitted to the West Vernon Convalescent Home in Los Angeles, where he died on March 16, 1975. He was inducted into the Blues Foundation Hall of Fame in 1980 and the Rock and Roll Hall of Fame in 1987.

* * * * *

According to author Mike Rowe, California's blues were a marriage of the Texas guitar to the urban jump blues of the 1940s, while Chicago's purer and more traditional style was the offspring of the Mississippi blues. The modern Delta style took root in Chicago because of the vast influx of Mississippi migrants during the 1940s; in fact, out of the total net migration to Chicago for these years it's probable that one-half came from Mississippi alone. A popular stop along the way was Memphis, Tennessee.

Albert Collins (1932-1993)

The "Master of the Telecaster," as he became known, Albert Collins was heavily influenced by T-Bone Walker and B.B. King, and took their styles to the next stage, bringing electric blues into a new era in the process.

Albert Collins was born in Leona, Texas, on October 3, 1932, and seldom ventured beyond Houston, where his family moved in 1939. It was there that his interest in music was sparked when he first heard the recordings of Louis Jordan and Jimmie Lunceford, who were very popular at the time. While in high school he took private piano lessons, but gave these up in favor of the guitar by the age of fourteen. Collins was further encouraged by Willow Young, an older cousin and friend of Houston blues legend Lightnin' Hopkins. Young taught Collins the rudiments of guitar, including the open E-minor tuning Collins always used.

Collins' first guitar was typical of a poor black teenager of the time: a cigarbox with a makeshift neck and strings of baling wire. He always kept the first real guitar he ever owned. It was made for him in exchange for yardwork by a carpenter who fashioned it out of oak, adding real rattlesnake rattles inside the body to improve its resonance. It was on this guitar that Collins first tried to imitate what he heard on the records of T-Bone Walker and Gatemouth Brown, two of his favorite performers.

By the time he was sixteen Collins had become proficient enough to form his own small band, and the trio of guitar, piano, and drums (a bassist was added about six months later) played at a Houston nightclub operated by friends of the family for more than a year. Collins was already playing an amplified guitar by then, but he mostly played Lightnin' Hopkins tunes because that's what his audience wanted to hear at the time.

Texas-style blues bands, perhaps reflecting the enormity of the state itself, were generally large, and bluesmen from the area were accustomed to the tradition of big bands with horn sections. Collins felt that if he observed this tradition he would be better able to generate a following of his own. So he left Houston for the Manhattan Club in Galveston, where—with the help of saxophonist Bobby Scott—over the next two years he added horns to his guitar-led rhythm section.

In the early 1950s Collins took to the road with singer Piney Brown, a period during which

Influenced by T-Bone Walker and Clarence "Gatemouth" Brown, the distinctive "cool" sound of Albert Collins' guitar first surfaced in 1958 on the instrumental "The Freeze," followed by "DeFrost" in 1960 and "Frosty" in 1962.

Collins felt he really began to develop as a musician. The tour took him through Texas, Louisiana, and Mississippi, with the final six months spent in New Orleans. Coming into contact with bluesmen from all over the deep South helped broaden his outlook as a musician, and as he absorbed other styles he created a unique, individual approach.

By the time he returned to Houston in 1954, the "frosty" guitar style typical of Albert Collins was becoming evident. He spent the next few years developing his style and honing his skills while keeping his band together between various day jobs. In 1958 he cut his first record, "The Freeze" b/w "Collins' Shuffle," the success of which enabled him to pursue his music full time. Two years later he recorded "DeFrost" and recorded and performed steadily ever after.

Ice Pickin' (1978), his first album for the Alligator label, was recorded with Larry Burton (second guitar), Aaron Burton (bass), and Casey Jones (drums). His last release, in 1991, was a self-titled debut for the Point Blank–Charisma label.

With a thriving port and railway connection, Memphis, Tennessee, was the murder capital of the world at the turn of the twentieth century and maintained its dicey reputation into the 1920s, when Beale Street became the epicenter of blues recording and performing.

Memphis Blues

A great number of musicians, drinkers, gamblers, swindlers, and prostitutes met in the clubs on Beale Street until late into the night. The most famous club on Beale Street, PeeWee's, had a sign with the following biting humor: "We do not close before the first murder."

—Gerard Herzhaft

The Delta may be known as the birthplace of the blues, but Memphis, at least since the days of William Christopher Handy, is known as the "Home of the Blues." Describing the black man whom he first witnessed singing the blues, Handy remarked that in his face was "the sadness of the ages."

In 1912 Handy published his first blues composition, "Memphis Blues," followed by "St Louis Blues," which carried the blues all over the world in 1914. In the 1920s, before Chicago began to dominate the industry, Memphis was a recording hub for the blues. Throughout the 1930s and 1940s, Beale Street was the center of a thriving blues scene.

Reacting to the popularity of KFFA's *King Biscuit Time*, by the late 1940s other radio stations in the area began to broadcast blues programs, particularly West Memphis, Arkansas, station KWEM and Memphis station WDIA. In 1948 Howlin' Wolf began broadcasting on KWEM with an electric blues band.

Howlin' Wolf (1910–1976)

A large, intimidating man who stood well over six feet [195cm] tall and weighed close to three hundred pounds [136kg], Wolf's gripping histrionics and sheer physical intensity gave new meaning to the blues nearly every time he performed.
—Robert Santelli

The Wolf was both a guitarist and harp player (he learned to play the harp from Sonny Boy Williamson), often playing both at the same time, keeping the harp close to his mouth with the aid of a harmonica rack. Born Chester Arthur Burnett (named after the late-nineteenth-century American president) on June 10, 1910, in either Aberdeen or West Point, Mississippi (he has given both locations as his birthplace), Burnett's Wolf persona may have had its roots in his childhood. His grandfather would tell him frightening tales of wolves, and his family took to threatening to "put the wolf" on him if he misbehaved.

The Wolf was thirteen when the blues found him on Young and Morrow's plantation, near Ruleville, where his parents moved in 1923. Will Dockery's plantation, also near Ruleville, was home to Charley Patton (1891–1934), whom the young Wolf would watch and listen to when the legendary bluesman toured neighboring plantations after cotton harvesting time. Known on Dockery's as "Bull Cow" and "Foot" for the size of his feet, Howlin' Wolf received his first guitar lessons from Patton himself during these frequent visits to the plantation.

In 1933 Howlin' Wolf's family crossed the Mississippi and moved to the Phillips plantation, about sixteen miles (26km) north of Parkin, Arkansas. Howlin' Wolf became interested in the harmonica upon meeting Sonny Boy Williamson #2, who later married Wolf's stepsister Mary. The two men met Robert Johnson in Robinsonville and hit the road as a trio for a while, playing in and around places like Itta Bena, Greenwood, and Moorhead. Wolf continued to divide his time playing the blues and working on his father's farm until 1941, when he was drafted into the army and shipped to Seattle for four years of duty.

Upon his release from the army, Wolf returned to his father's farm on the Phillips plantation before starting his own farm in Penton, Mississippi. There he raised a couple of crops and started playing again, this time with Fiddling Joe Martin and Woodrow Adams, around nearby Robinsonville and Tunica. As music began to occupy more and more of his time (he was playing electric guitar and harmonica by then), he left the farm and moved to West Memphis.

In 1948 Howlin' Wolf formed a band with guitarists Pat Hare (1930–1980) and Matt "Guitar" Murphy (b. 1929), West Memphis native and harp player Junior Parker (1932–1971), a drummer named Willie Steele, and a piano player who was known only as "Destruction." Guitarist Willie Johnson joined the band when Matt Murphy and Junior Parker left to form the Blue Flames; together with the remaining members, Howlin' Wolf toured throughout Arkansas and Mississippi. Wolf's own distinct style was already emerging at this point, as he would leap onto the stage announcing himself as "Big Foot Chester" and follow with a series of fierce howls.

Following Sonny Boy (Rice Miller) Williamson's lead, Howlin' Wolf—pictured with his National guitar at the grand opening of a grocery store in West Memphis—achieved great local popularity hosting his own show, beginning in 1948, on radio station KWEM in West Memphis, Arkansas. Just a few years later, in 1952, he would record the seminal "How Many More Years" for Sam Phillips.

The band's big break came when they landed a spot on radio station KWEM in West Memphis. Wolf's popularity earned him a position as an announcer for a program designed to draw agricultural advertising sponsors, a job he held until leaving for Chicago. It was during these broadcasts that he first called himself "Howlin' Wolf."

In 1950 Sam Phillips was recording blues artists in his Memphis studio for the Bihari brothers' Hollywood-based Modern label. At the time, Ike Turner (b. 1931) was signed to Phillips' own label, Sun Records, until a conflict of interest arose between Phillips and Modern Records over Turner's participation in a B.B. King recording session. Turner had caught the attention of Jules Bihari, who subsequently insisted that the Clarksdale pianist play on King's tracks despite Turner's contract with the Sun label. Further raising the ire of Sam Phillips, Bihari actually offered Turner a job as talent scout for Modern Records.

It was Ike Turner, in his capacity as talent scout for the Bihari brothers, who discovered the Wolf. Assuming business as usual, Jules Bihari sent a contract and arranged for Howlin' Wolf's recording session at the Sun Records studio. But Sam Phillips exacted his revenge for the earlier insult by sending the Wolf masters to Chess Records in Chicago. These first sides by the future blues legend, "How Many More Years" b/w "Moanin' At Midnight," were an immediate success upon their release on August 15, 1951.

Howlin' Wolf, pictured with (from left to right) Chess session musician Jody Williams, Chicago blues drummer Earl Phillips, and loyal sideman Hubert Sumlin (who stopped playing for two years after being devastated by Wolf's death in 1976), quickly became an integral part of the Chicago blues scene shortly after his arrival in the Windy City in 1954.

"I was a farmer and I didn't know what was happening. I was glad to get a sound out, y'know," was how the Wolf described the wheelings and dealings within the record industry. With roots that ran deep in the rich soil of Delta cottonfields, Howlin' Wolf was understandably bewildered by the tug of war that ensued between big-city recording companies Modern and Chess.

Howlin' Wolf moved to Chicago in autumn of 1952. Off to a slow start, he did not record at all during his first year and played only sporadic gigs at places like the Rock Bottom and Club Zanzibar. Early in 1954 Wolf made his first recordings for Chess Records, "I Love My Baby" and "All Night Long." Backed by the studio's house musicians for the session, he decided soon afterward to return to the South and try to regroup his band. Willie Johnson and Hubert Sumlin (b. 1931) agreed to make the trip, but Willie Steele was already in the army. Wolf's first release following the reunion, "No Place to Go," was described by *Cash Box* magazine in May 1954 as "an overnight hit," and by June the song had reached number two on the magazine's R&B chart in Memphis. A few years later, in 1960, the enigmatic "Spoonful" was recorded for Chess in Chicago with Otis Spann (piano), Hubert Sumlin (guitar), Willie Dixon (bass), and Fred Below (drums).

Howlin' Wolf was a contemporary and often a rival of Muddy Waters while they were both signed with Chess Records in Chicago, and it has been argued that the competition between the two blues legends inspired them both to rise to new heights. The Wolf's final performance was in Chicago with B.B. King in November 1975. He died from kidney failure two months later. Howlin' Wolf was inducted into the Blues Foundation Hall of Fame in 1980 and the Rock and Roll Hall of Fame in 1991.

B.B. King (b. 1925)

The blues are almost sacred to some people, but others don't understand, and when I can't make them understand, it makes me feel bad, because they mean so much to me....

—B.B. King

Born Riley B. King in Indianola, Mississippi, King received the nickname "Blues Boy" (later shortened to "B.B.") from time spent on Beale Street while working as a disc jockey for radio station WDIA in Memphis. He has since become the blues' most successful concert artist and has been bestowed with more awards than any other bluesman, confirming his place as an elder statesman and ambassador of the blues. King is also among the most eloquent and gracious when discussing the significance of America's indigenous music and has played a major role in bringing it widespread respect and admiration.

The reverence he holds for the blues is all over the face of a young B.B. King, pictured here with his beloved Lucille at the recording studios of ABC-Paramount in the 1960s.

When his father caught up with him at the age of fourteen and insisted that B.B. King live with an aunt, the "Beale Street Blues Boy" had been supporting himself following his mother's death six years before; by the age of twelve, King owned his own mule and plow. The blues legend works just as hard at this writing, averaging three hundred performances a year.

King's earliest musical interests were formed in church, where he sang gospel and was introduced to the guitar by—as unlikely as it may seem—a minister. His sophisticated style of blues guitar can be traced to the influences of such jazzmen as Charlie Christian and Django Reinhardt (1910–1953), and the big-band sounds of Duke Ellington and Count Basie. In addition, strains of the traditional Delta/Texas styles of T-Bone Walker and Lonnie Johnson are also evident. An accomplished master of a guitar technique known as string-bending (also a hallmark of Albert King), B.B. became a profound influence on many rock guitarists, including Eric Clapton, Jeff Beck (b. 1944), Jimmy Page (b. 1944), and Johnny Winter (b. 1944).

Following World War II, King left the Delta for Memphis, where he stayed with his cousin Bukka White (1909–1977). After hearing Sonny Boy Williamson on the radio, King went to West Memphis to request work from Williamson on KWEM. His performance on *King Biscuit Time* led to a full-time position as a disc jockey on WDIA in 1949. King's popularity on WDIA led to numerous club dates in Beale Street's blues clubs, where he often shared the stage with Robert "Junior" Lockwood, Rosco Gordon (b. 1934), Bobby "Blue" Bland (b. 1930), and Johnny Ace (1929–1954), among others.

A prolific recording career began quietly in 1949 with four sides waxed for the Nashville-based Bullet label that left little impression. In 1952, however, King's release of "Three O'Clock Blues" on the Modern label went to number one on the newly formed R&B charts ("Rhythm & Blues" replaced "Race Records" on *Billboard*'s charts in 1949) and stayed there for seventeen weeks. On the heels of his chart success, King toured extensively throughout the mid-1950s; in 1956 alone he reputedly performed 342 shows. His widespread popularity enabled him to pull the blues out of backwater obscurity and ghetto isolation into the limelight of mainstream admiration.

Albert King (1923-1992)

The "Velvet Bulldozer" was born Albert Nelson on April 25, 1923, in Indianola, Mississippi, and was among the first of the major blues guitarists to gain crossover success. Playing his distinctive Gibson Flying V upside down, the left-handed King had one of the most recognizable guitar styles in the blues, using his instrument in the call-and-response style common to gospel and some blues.

King built his first diddley bow—the primal instrument for a majority of blues guitarists—at the age of six, upgrading to the cigar-box model after seeing Blind Lemon Jefferson perform live for the first time around Forest City, Arkansas, in the late 1930s. King acquired his first acoustic guitar at eighteen; he flipped the guitar over and became self-taught in the style of T-Bone Walker, one of the most popular blues guitarists in the 1940s. By 1950 King had saved enough for an electric axe through construction work in the Little Rock and Osceola area.

Shortly afterward King formed the In the Groove Boys with Eddie Snow (piano) and Odell Mitchell (drums), and was featured on radio station KOSE in Osceola. Still feeling his way about musically, however, King left the group around 1952 and joined a gospel quartet, the Harmony Kings. He stopped playing guitar altogether for a while and ended up backing Jimmy Reed on drums for a short stint in Gary, Indiana, before going to Chicago in 1953 to record for the Parrot label.

Around 1956 King relocated to St. Louis, eventually landing a contract with the local Bobbin label in 1956. With the help of an outstanding production team that included Ike Turner, King slowly came into a style of his own and recorded a number of fine blues through 1963, including 1961's "This Morning," made in response to the Mar-Keys' instrumental "Last Night." Emblematic of the social forces taking hold in the United States, the Mar-Keys were a biracial group that evolved from the house musicians at Memphis' Stax Records, the label that would become the source for some of the finest soul music to be heard in the 1960s.

King signed on with Stax in 1966 and was teamed with the funky instrumental soul group Booker T. & the MG's, gaining a receptive crossover audience for the next ten years, until the label folded. "Laundromat Blues" was recorded for Stax Records in Memphis in 1966 with Booker T. (piano, electric bass) and Al Jackson (drums), followed by the classic album *Born Under a Bad Sign* in 1967.

In 1968, Albert King was the first blues artist to perform at rock's legendary venue in San Francisco, the Fillmore West, where he shared the stage with John Mayall and fellow left-hander Jimi Hendrix on opening night. The following year he performed with the St. Louis Symphony, briefly bringing together the blues and classical music. A fallow period ensued from the mid-1970s through most of the 1980s, during which time King often threatened to retire for good, only to return by popular demand.

Albert King was inducted into the Blues Foundation's Hall of Fame in 1983, and continued to tour, often with B.B. King, throughout the 1980s. Albert King was about to embark on a major European tour before he succumbed to a heart attack in 1992.

Albert King, pictured here playing his original issue Gibson Flying V upside down and backwards, had one of the most distinctive guitar voices in the blues, emulated by the likes of Stevie Ray Vaughan and Jimi Hendrix.

Memphis Blues

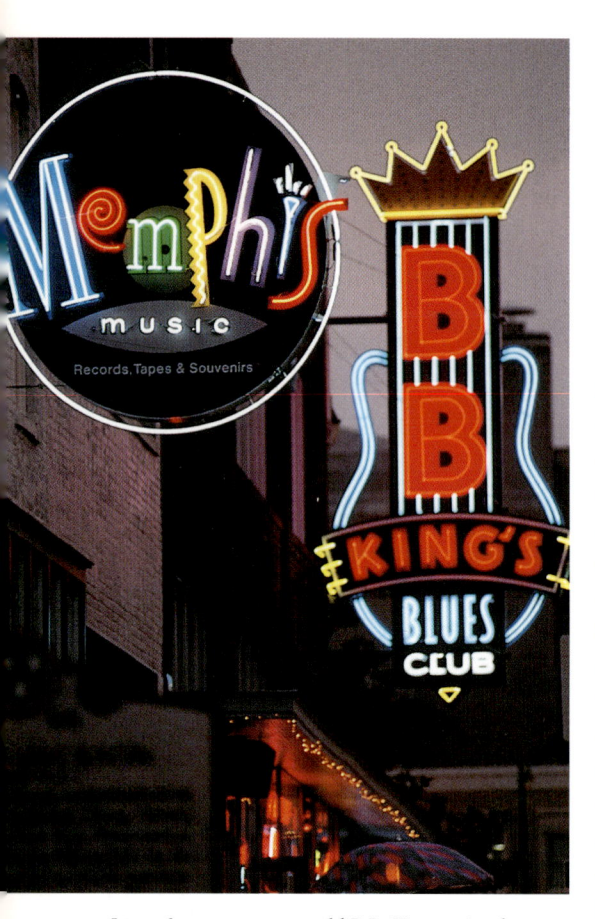

In 1946 a twenty-year-old B.B. King arrived on Beale Street with $2.50 in his pocket. He returned in 1991 and opened B.B. King's Blues Club and Restaurant at 143 Beale Street, where audiences can hear regular performers Ruby Wilson & the King B's while chowing down on a Lucille burger or a King steak and topping it all off with a slice of Bluesberry cheesecake.

"Everyday I Have the Blues" was written in the 1930s by Aaron and Milton Sparks in St. Louis. Aaron "Pinetop" Sparks was the first to record the tune—on July 28, 1935, for the Bluebird label. It was also recorded by guitarist Lowell Fulson and pianist Lloyd Glenn (1909–1985) on July 18, 1949, and became a hit for the Swingtime label. King, who had become known for breathing new life into old standards, made the song a hit again in 1955. He also recorded an outstanding live version at the Regal in Chicago on November 21, 1964, with Johnny Board (tenor sax), Bobby Forte (tenor sax), Kenny Sands (trumpet), Duke Jethro (organ), Leo Lauchie (electric bass), and Sonny Freeman (drums).

B.B. King gained a new audience, namely rock fans, in the late 1960s, and he began playing rock festivals and at such rock venues as the Fillmore East and West and opening for bands like the Rolling Stones. He crossed over with "The Thrill Is Gone," which made it to number fifteen on the pop charts in 1970. For the remainder of the decade King and his beloved guitar, Lucille, toured regularly throughout the United States and Europe.

King took his rightful place in the Blues Foundation's Hall of Fame in 1980 and the Rock and Roll Hall of Fame in 1987. In 1988 he appeared on Irish supergroup U2's album *Rattle and Hum*, bringing a gospel/blues feel to the hit "When Love Comes to Town."

* * * * *

As had B.B. King and so many other blues legends, John Lee Hooker started out on Beale Street, where at around the age of fifteen he worked as an usher at the New Daisy theater and busked with his guitar on street corners. However, he made his mark in Detroit, where he had gone in search of work on the assembly line in the height of the production boom during World War II. In December 1950 the formation of the Chance label, located at 2011 S. Michigan Avenue, was announced by record producer Art Sheridan. The first of the new country blues artists to record for the label was Hooker, soon to gain a reputation as "Father of the Boogie."

John Lee Hooker (b. 1917)

You had to play electric in those clubs, they were so noisy. —John Lee Hooker

Originally from Clarksdale, Mississippi, in the heart of the Delta, John Lee Hooker was influenced by the likes of T-Bone Walker, Blind Lemon Jefferson, and Charley Patton. He later moved to Detroit and became the Motor City's biggest blues star from the 1940s to 1950s. Hooker became known as the "Father of the Boogie" after the release of his 1948 hit for the Modern label, "Boogie Chillen'," his first recording using an electric guitar. Hooker went on to perform and record at least twenty different versions of the tune. Written by Hooker, "Boogie Chillen'" was a free adaptation of the folk piece "Mama Don't Allow Me to Stay Out All Night Long."

Born in Clarksdale on August 22, 1917, Hooker learned to play the guitar from his stepfather, Will Moore, and left for

John Lee Hooker remains one of the most prolific (not to mention confusing) recording artists in the history of the blues with nearly as many pseudonyms as titles, including "Texas Slim," on the King label; "Birmingham Sam," for Regent; "Johnny Williams," with Gotham; and "John Lee Booker," on the Chance, Acorn, Deluxe, Gone, and Rockin' labels in 1951 alone.

Memphis Blues

John Lee Hooker, "the Boogie Man," has more than four hundred titles to his credit, so he knows what he's talking about when he sings in "Teaching the Blues": "Fancy chords don't mean nothin'/... Get this beat...this slow beat...this big beat...."

Memphis to play the blues at the age of fourteen. By time he was seventeen he was performing with slide guitarist Robert Nighthawk and playing house parties with B.B. King and Bobby "Blue" Bland. At eighteen Hooker relocated again, first to Cincinnati for three years, and then in 1943 to the Motor City, where he worked on an assembly line during the day while playing house parties at night. It was at one of those house parties that Hooker drew the attention of record producers Bernie Besman and Elmer Barber.

Originally recorded for the Sensation label and distributed by Modern Records, "Boogie Chillen'" created an overnight sensation, enabling Hooker to quit his day job and concentrate on his blues. Hooker recorded for numerous labels under as many names, making him one of the most recorded bluesmen of all time. He has also played with the best in the blues and beyond, including his cousin Earl Hooker (1930–1970), Eddie Taylor, Jimmy Reed, T-Bone Walker, Willie Dixon, Otis Spann, Muddy Waters, Wayne Bennett, Phil Upchurch, Lowell Fulson, Robert Cray (b. 1953), Charlie Musselwhite (b. 1944), Bonnie Raitt (b. 1949), Carlos Santana (b. 1947), Los Lobos, and Steve Miller (b. 1943).

In the early 1960s Hooker influenced an entire generation of British blues rockers, including the Animals, Rolling Stones, John Mayall's Bluesbreakers, and the early Fleetwood Mac. Stateside, he gained a new following after performing at the 1960 Newport Folk Festival in Rhode Island. In addition, Canned Heat (with whom he toured and recorded an album in 1971), Johnny Winter, and George Thorogood (b. 1951) have all borrowed extensively from the Hooker catalog.

Hooker was awarded a Grammy for best blues recording for his album *The Healer* (on which longtime fan Bonnie Raitt made an appearance) in 1989 and was inducted into the Rock and Roll Hall of Fame in 1990. Hooker currently lives in Los Angeles and continues to electrify audiences to this day.

* * * * *

In addition to Hooker, others from the Delta region who began their recording careers in the 1940s and 1950s included Arthur "Big Boy" Crudup (1905–1974), Big Walter Horton (1917–1981), Sunnyland Slim (1907–?), Johnny Shines (1915–1992), and Hound Dog Taylor (1917–1975), to name just a few. During the 1950s these leaders and their sidemen settled in Chicago, where they contributed to the development of "urban blues." According to Gerard Herzhaft, "The Chicago blues of the fifties is, in fact, an extension and an electrification of the Delta blues."

Sweet Home Chicago

The two main features of black life in the United States were segregation and migration; the former providing impetus for the latter.

—Mike Rowe

The next great wave of African American migration took place after World War II. Though they had proved their courage and dedication to their nation while overseas and had made the ultimate sacrifice in the "war to make the world safe for democracy," African Americans discovered that despite their valor, little about the twin evils of racism and segregation had changed in the United States. Riding the rails when they could or walking the highways, African American migrants generally followed the most direct route out of the South: some left the eastern seaboard states of Georgia, Alabama, and the Carolinas for New York; natives of Mississippi, Arkansas, and other states of the Deep South left for Chicago and Detroit; and those from Texas and sections of Arkansas, Oklahoma, and Missouri made their way to San Francisco and Los Angeles.

Figuring prominently in many blues compositions, Highways 51 and 61—in conjunction with the Illinois Central—carried innumerable Delta bluesmen north to St. Louis and Chicago, where they hoped to find better employment than they could back home. Census statistics for the period reveal that from 1955 to 1960, 60 percent of African American migrants to Chicago were Mississippi-born. This led to severe overcrowding in the predominantly black Cook County of Chicago, a surviving example of which is the storefront church so commonplace to the South Side. African Americans of the South were born with the blues, a tradition they did not relinquish when they went north. The next generation of bluesmen born in Chicago or brought there as children joined with their counterparts from the South in creating a "gospel-tinged, jazz-inflected, Delta-derived Chicago blues."

Following the recording ban issued during the raw-materials shortage of World War II, small independent companies, called (then as now) "indies," entered the industry to compete with the major companies for a newly expanding market. Since the leading bluesmen were under contract to the majors, the indies had to seek new talent, who in turn brought new sounds into the recording studios, which naturally spilled over into the clubs. The music of this period is generally referred to as "urban blues." The blues of the city became electrified, its distinctive features amplified guitars, harmonicas, and a full-blown blues band—which added drums, piano, and horns to the traditional guitar or harmonica accompaniment.

The sound of Chicago blues before 1945 was epitomized by the jazz-tinged "Bluebird beat," named for the market domination of the "race" catalogs of RCA/Bluebird and Columbia. A long-time admirer of jazz, Lester

Sweet Home Chicago

Chicago replaced Memphis as the undisputed "Home of the Blues" (with the help of harpist John Lee "Sonny Boy" Williamson) in the late 1940s and early 1950s and remains as such today. The skyline of the Windy City along Lake Shore Drive is pictured here from across Lake Michigan.

Melrose—the producer who oversaw the Bluebird and Columbia catalogs—had produced Jerry Roll Morton (1890–1941) and King Oliver (1885–1938) in the 1920s, followed by the Hokum Boys toward the end of the decade. In 1930 Melrose discovered and produced the recordings of Big Bill Broonzy (1897–1958). He also recorded Muddy Waters in 1946, but failing to recognize the original talent of the future blues legend, Melrose allowed the recordings to remain unreleased until 1971.

Muddy Waters (1915–1983)

They call me Muddy Waters/I'm just restless, man, as the deep blue sea.
—Muddy Waters

Tutored by Delta bluesman Eddie James "Son" House, Jr. (1902–1988), and influenced by Robert Johnson (who also learned much from Son House) and Charley Patton, Muddy Waters in turn became one of the most influential people in the history of electric blues and a primary shaper of the post–World War II Chicago blues sound.

Born McKinley Morganfield on April 4, 1915, in Rolling Fork, Mississippi, the young Waters earned his nickname playing in the silty waters of Deer Creek, near his father Ollie Morganfield's shotgun shack. His mother Berta died when Muddy was three, and he was subsequently raised by his grandmother Della Jones on Stovall's plantation, just outside Clarksdale and 95 miles (152km) north of Rolling Fork along Highway 61. Like many of his ancestors before him (including his father, who was a sharecropper), Waters learned to sing while working in the cotton fields, where he earned fifty cents a day. He picked up his first harmonica when he was around twelve or thirteen years old and learned to play guitar at about the age of seventeen. By 1932 he was playing the local jukes and fish-fries in the area.

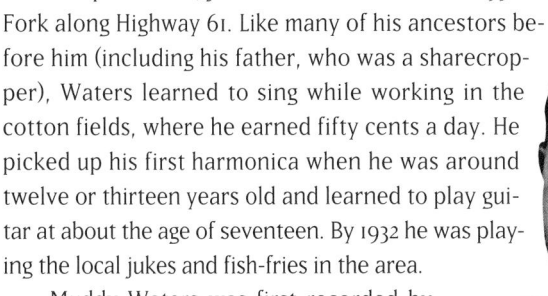

Muddy Waters was first recorded by folklorist Alan Lomax for the Library of Congress in 1941 and 1942. Lomax was in search of the legacy of Robert Johnson and was directed to the young Muddy Waters, who played in the style of the King of Delta Blues. Two of the songs from a session on Stovall's plantation, "Country Blues" and "I Be's Troubled," were included on a Library of Congress folk anthology album and whetted Waters' appetite for recording.

"I'd never heard my voice. But when Mr. Lomax played me the record I thought, man, this boy can sing the blues. And I was surprised because I didn't know I sang like that" (Muddy Waters to Paul Oliver).

Waters left Clarksdale for Chicago in May 1943, changing trains in Memphis for the Illinois Central. In Chicago Big Bill Broonzy helped him break into the blues scene that was flourishing on the South Side. He started performing with John Lee "Sonny Boy" Williamson (1914–1948), playing acoustic guitar behind the blues harpist. Finding he could not compete with the volume of the average Chicago blues bar, Waters bought a cheap electric guitar in 1944. In 1945 he teamed up with guitarist and harpist Jimmy Rogers, guitarist Claude Smith, and later with pianist Eddie Boyd (1914–?) followed by Sunnyland Slim. Waters still played in the traditional Delta bottleneck style, but he was developing a richer, more intense sound that grew in tandem with the relatively new electric guitar medium.

Waters recorded with a five-piece band for producer Lester Melrose of Columbia Records in 1946. The following year he recorded behind Sunnyland Slim on "Johnson Machine Gun" and "Fly Right Little Girl" for the Chess subsidiary label Aristocrat. "Hard Day Blues" was recorded for Columbia Records in Chicago on September 27, 1947. He also recorded "Gypsy Woman" and "Little Anna Mae" with bass player Big Crawford. In 1948 Leonard Chess brought Waters and Crawford back into the studio, where they recorded "I Can't Be Satisfied" b/w "Feel Like Going Home," which were released as an Aristocrat single. Although both cuts were in the traditional Delta style, Waters' slashing electric slide guitar brought a new edge to the sound, and the single's entire stock was sold out in less than a day. Waters gave his audience (largely transplanted Southerners

Jimmy Rogers (b. 1924)

One of Grozie Lane and Henry Rogers' ten children, Jimmy Rogers was born James A. Lane in Atlanta, Georgia, on June 3, 1924. He was raised by his maternal grandmother, Leanna Jackson, and spent most of his early childhood in and around Ruleville, Atlanta, and Memphis. Probably inspired by Sonny Boy Williamson's show on KFFA, the young Rogers taught himself to play the harmonica while in Atlanta.

Also inspired by the records of Big Bill Broonzy, Memphis Minnie, and later Arthur "Big Boy" Crudup and Louis Jordan, Rogers' first guitar was the traditional one-string, or "diddley bow," which he made from broom wire around 1935. In Memphis he was inspired by guitarists Joe Willie Wilkins, Robert Nighthawk, and Robert "Junior" Lockwood, and by 1940 was proficient enough to play at local house parties in Mississippi.

While in Phillip, Mississippi, Rogers met Sonny Boy Williamson and his band, which at the time included Joe Wilkins, Dudlow Taylor, and Peck Curtis. One night Williamson invited Rogers to sit in for Joe Wilkins on guitar. Soon afterwards, Rogers left Mississippi for West Memphis, where he met Howlin' Wolf and Sunnyland Slim. After about a year, he went up to St. Louis with Slim for about six months before moving on to Chicago, where he had a great-uncle.

While in the Windy City Rogers met and began playing second guitar with Muddy Waters, with whom he stayed from around 1950 to 1956, seminal years in the forging of Chicago blues. On August 15, 1950, Jimmy Rogers' first hit, "That's All Right," recorded with Little Walter and Big Crawford, was released by Chess Records. The success of that record established Jimmy Rogers as an important bluesman in his own right and he began recording regularly under his own name (although still backed by Waters' band). In contrast to Muddy Waters' often dark and ominous sound, Rogers was upbeat and polished, which inspired Len Chess to release his records under the name Jimmy Rogers and his Rocking Four.

In January 1951 Rogers formed his own band with Eddie Ware on piano and Ernest Cotton on tenor saxophone. Little Walter replaced Ernest Cotton's saxophone with his guitar and harp in July of the same year (notably one of the few times Walter, known for his harp, played guitar).

Rogers went solo in 1956 and was replaced by Auburn "Pat" Hare early in 1957. For the remainder of the decade Rogers released a handful of nominally successful singles and worked as a sideman with Howlin' Wolf and Sonny Boy Williamson before retiring from the music business in the 1960s.

In 1971 he returned to the blues scene, often performing with Johnny Littlejohn. Rogers continued to record and perform through the 1980s and released two albums for the French Black & Blue label. The album *Ludella*, on which Rogers was backed by Kim Wilson, Pinetop Perkins, and Hubert Sumlin, was released on the Antone label and remains one of his finest efforts to date.

Pioneering electric blues guitarist Jimmy Rogers, pictured here at the 1995 Brecon Jazz Festival, is credited with encouraging Muddy Waters to amplify his guitar shortly after the two met in the mid-1940s.

Sweet Home Chicago

like himself) the down-home sounds they were missing wrapped in an urban sensibility—the result was the Chess brothers' first commercial success and the recipe for many more to come.

At this time Waters was performing in Chicago clubs with a full band that featured Jimmy Rogers on second guitar and harmonica and "Baby Face" Leroy Foster on drums and guitar (Little Walter Jacobs would join him on harmonica a little later). But Leonard Chess, relying on the direct evidence of previous success, insisted on keeping the lineup of Crawford and Waters the same. It was not until 1950 that Waters had the opportunity to record with a full band. His first release on the Chess label, "Rollin' Stone" b/w "Walkin' Blues," was a nationwide hit.

By 1954 Muddy Waters had practically laid his guitar aside, instead concentrating on vocals and fronting his band. The shift was indicative of his turning away from traditional Delta blues toward the more urban format befitting a Chicago bluesman. Consequently "Hoochie Coochie Man," his first release of 1954, was a rocking success and his best seller to date.

Tragedy struck the Waters' band in June that same year when harp-player Henry Strong (1928–1954) was murdered. Together with Otis Spann, Elgin Evans, and Jimmy Rogers, Strong had been a touring member of the "best blues band in the world" for two years, and was close friends with harp legend "Little" Walter Jacobs (1930–1968), who described the young harp player as "the best harp-blower in Chicago next to me."

Muddy Waters firmly established his reputation in Chicago when he debuted at Sylvio's in 1947, following in the footsteps of "Big" Maceo Merriwether, Tampa Red, Big Bill Broonzy, Sonny Boy Williamson, and other blues legends who made their names at one of Chicago's best-known blues clubs.

"When I sing the blues, when I'm singing the real blues, I'm singing what I feel. Some people maybe want to laugh; maybe I don't talk so good and they don't understand y'know? But...when I sing the blues it comes from the heart" (Muddy Waters to Paul Oliver).

Big Walter Horton (c.1917–1981) had introduced Strong to Muddy Waters as Horton's replacement for a date at Club Zanzibar in 1952, and Strong passed the audition. Sadly, his tenure would be cut short. In the early morning hours of June 3 he was stabbed to death in his home following an argument with the woman he was seeing at the time, leaving Little Walter to lament that "Last night I lost the best friend I ever had."

Although Strong never recorded with Waters (Len Chess maintained creative control over the personnel in his studio, and Little Walter was a ubiquitous presence), Waters nonetheless found it difficult to replace him in the touring band. "Little" George Smith joined just long enough to see Waters through his tour dates for the remainder of the year, from Birmingham to Arkansas, back up to Detroit, then four months on the road, and ending finally in Los Angeles. James Cotton (b. 1935) eventually replaced Smith following the tour, completing the lineup, which consisted of pianist Otis Spann, guitarist Pat Hare, and either Francis Clay or Willie Smith on drums.

A powerful songwriter, interpreter, and performer as well as an outstanding bandleader, Waters has shared the stage with some of the greats of the Chicago blues scene. His band has included guitarists Pat Hare (1930–1980), Luther Tucker (1936–1993), and Earl Hooker; harp players Little Walter, Junior Wells (b. 1934), and Carey Bell (b. 1936); bass players Big Crawford and Willie Dixon; piano players Memphis Slim (1915–1988) and Pinetop Perkins (b. 1913); and drummers Elgin Evans, Fred Below (1926–1988), and Francis Clay (b. 1923), to name just a few.

From 1951 to 1960, there was not a finer blues band in the world than the Muddy Waters Blues Band, and few bluesmen, save Little Walter, could compete with Waters in Chicago. The recordings produced during this seminal period included the Waters originals "Long Distance Call," "Mannish Boy," "Got My Mojo Working," and "She Moves Me"; Willie Dixon's vital contributions included "Hoochie Coochie Man," "I'm Ready," and "I Just Want to Make Love to You," among others. *The Best of Muddy Waters,* a collection of hit singles that was also his debut album (as opposed to the numerous singles) for the Chess label, was released in 1957, the year before Waters toured England with pianist Otis Spann.

Muddy Waters became the link between traditional Delta blues and the electric blues that developed in Chicago after World War II, in turn becoming the driving force behind rock and roll. Although lacking a formal education, Waters spoke about the blues with a simple eloquence and dignity that brought newfound respect to the music.

Muddy Waters died in his sleep of a heart attack in Chicago on April 30, 1983. He had taken his rightful place in the Blues Foundation Hall of Fame in 1980 and was inducted into the Rock and Roll Hall of Fame in 1987.

* * * * *

Brothers Phil and Leonard Chess emigrated to the United States from Poland in 1928 and settled on South Karlov street in Chicago's Jewish district. By 1937 they owned a small chain of bars and shops in the predominantly black South Side of Chicago. Among the most successful was The Macomba Club on 39th and Cottage Grove, where artists like Billy Eckstine, Ella Fitzgerald, Gene Ammons, and Jump Jackson performed fairly regularly.

Leonard Chess, inspired by the obvious demand for recordings of—and lack of recording facilities for—new jump blues and jazz artists, decided together with his brother Phil and an outside partner to start a recording company, Aristocrat Records, around 1947. The fledgling label started out in a small office at 71st and Phillips and was distributed from Diversey Avenue by James Martin. It did not take long, however, for demand to overwhelm the small outlet, and the brothers Chess took over their own distribution from a larger office at 5249 S. Cottage Grove.

By August of the same year *Billboard* magazine was carrying details of Chess' forthcoming releases: the label had signed Jump Jackson's Orchestra, the Dozier Boys, and the Five Blazes. In 1952 Aristocrat began a new life as Chess Records, followed shortly thereafter by subsidiaries Checker, Argo, and Cadet. The first issue by the new label was by Gene Ammons, and by 1954, with the help of promoter and disc jockey Alan Freed, Chess artists reigned over at least half of the newly christened R&B chart. A great deal of the success of Chess Records can be attributed to the talents of producers like Ralph Bass, Gene Barge, and Willie Dixon.

Described by Len Chess as his "right arm" and a fixture of the Chicago blues scene, Willie Dixon became Chess Record's leading talent scout, producer, composer, and session musician shortly after he joined the record company through its fledgling Aristocrat label in 1951.

Willie Dixon (1915-1992)

I am the blues. —Willie Dixon

From behind the scenes as well as on the stage, Willie Dixon (who was with Chess Records in the 1950s and 1960s) was essential to the shaping of postwar Chicago blues. There was little he did not do at Chess, spending his years there as a composer, producer, arranger, bass player, recording artist, talent scout, and bandleader, to name just a handful of the many hats he wore while with the label.

Willie Dixon was born on April 1, 1915, in Vicksburg, Mississippi, where his mother wrote and recited religious poetry. He sang gospel with the Union Jubilee Singers and learned to play the string bass as a boy, before his family moved to Chicago in 1935 or 1936.

Dixon initially pursued a boxing career shortly after his arrival in the Windy City, becoming the Illinois State Golden Gloves novice-division heavyweight champion a year later. Dixon showed promise as a fighter (he even sparred with Joe Louis), but a brawl with his manager over money effectively ended whatever boxing career he may have had.

Sweet Home Chicago

Dixon hung up his gloves for a stand-up bass in 1939, when he formed the Five Breezes with piano player Leonard "Baby Doo" Caston. The group achieved moderate success playing Chicago clubs and recorded for the Bluebird label in 1940. Then Dixon's career took an unexpected turn in 1941, when he was arrested as a conscientious objector for refusing to serve in the U.S. Armed Forces.

After the case was settled (in Dixon's favor), Dixon returned to Chicago's club scene with a new group, the Four Jumps of Jive, which recorded for Mercury Records in 1945. He was reunited with "Baby Doo" Caston the same year, and together with guitarist Bernardo Dennis (replaced by Ollie Crawford the following year), they formed the Big Three Trio early in 1946.

The group's jump style of blues in three-part harmony (unique for the blues, which does not easily lend itself to the kind of vocal approach popularized by doo-wop groups like the Moonglows) was very popular in Chicago's clubs, where they played for several months before recording for Jim Bulleit's Delta and Bullet labels. In 1947 they were compacted (together with the sides they had recorded for Bullet) to Lester Melrose of Columbia Records, where they remained until disbanding in December 1952. Dixon remembered those days fondly, remarking to Mary K. Aldin, associate editor of *Living Blues* magazine, that "this was before Chess, before none of that big blues stuff was happenin'....It was good times, you know."

Indeed, it could be argued that none of that "blues stuff" would have happened without Willie Dixon, who has been called the "Father of Modern Chicago Blues." The Big Three Trio, with its unique blend of blues, novelty tunes, and pop ballads, toured all over the country in those days, but always came home to Chicago, which is where Willie Dixon first met Len Chess.

The fact that Dixon's rise to fame should parallel the decline of blues may seem unusual at first, but when you consider that he was responsible for nearly all the blues to come out of Chicago at the time, it's understandable that the material would eventually start to stagnate. Dixon claimed to have written more than 250 songs, but as music historian Mike Rowe commented, "often the quantity [was] more evident than the quality." Like Lester Melrose, Dixon was almost *too* prolific, and his compositions began to sound the same.

Willie Dixon was inducted into the Blues Foundation's Hall of Fame in 1980. He died of a heart ailment in 1992.

From 1954 on, Willie Dixon was one of the leading house producers at Chess Records, arranging and often playing on dozens of sessions, including those of Robert Nighthawk, Muddy Waters, Howlin' Wolf, Little Walter, Chuck Berry, Buddy Guy, and Otis Rush.

Veteran bluesman Otis Rush is still going strong today, recently opening for Pearl Jam at Chicago's Soldier's Field.

The West Side

There's a thing with most of the West Side boys. What we're doing is playing with a bass, drums and guitar, but we're thinking of a horn or two horns and when we throw those heavy chords that's what we're doing.

—Jimmy Dawkins

The heavy guitar sound that bluesman Jimmy Dawkins (b. 1936) describes developed in part for economic reasons. In the dilapidated and overcrowded West Side of Chicago, there were few bands who could afford the horn section that gave much of the Chicago blues its characteristic hard-edged urban sound.

Early in 1956 Eli Toscano, together with partner Joe Brown, started the Abco label, the West Side's first record company. The fledgling label enjoyed only moderate success with releases by Louis Myers, Morris Pejoe, and Arbee Stidham, the first artists to join the roster. Joe Brown bowed out not long afterward, and Toscano formed his own label, Cobra Records, in August of the same year. By October Cobra had its first and only top-ten hit as "I Can't Quit You Baby" entered the charts. Written by Willie Dixon, it was recorded by a young man from Mississippi who had learned to play guitar only two years before: Otis Rush.

The West Side

Otis Rush (b. 1934)

Rush, especially, listened widely to other artists and other genres, building chords inspired by Jimmy Smith's organ technique and absorbing the tonal subtleties of jazz guitarists such as Kenny Burrell to produce his own individual blend.

—Paul Oliver

That Rush would become Cobra's most recorded bluesman probably surprised no one more than the guitarist himself. Born on April 29, 1934, in Philadelphia, Mississippi, he was playing around with a harmonica and listening to the records of Little Walter, Muddy Waters, and B.B. King by the time his family moved to Chicago in 1948. Rush found work in the stockyards, where he also found a friend, Mike Netton. Together they tried to form a band with Rush on harp and Netton playing drums.

Whatever success they may have had notwithstanding, Rush took up the guitar in 1954, no doubt inspired by his idol, B.B. King. Like Albert King, Rush was naturally left-handed and played a right-handed guitar upside down. He must have been a fast learner, for he acquired his first club date less than a year later. With "Poor Bob" Woodfork from Arkansas on second guitar, they played for Bob Jones at the Alibi club.

Around this time Willie Dixon had left Chess Records for Eli Toscano's new Cobra label, following one of the many disputes Dixon had with Len Chess over the years. Dixon remembered Rush, who had shown up at the Chess studios previously in an unsuccessful attempt to gain a recording contract. Dixon brought Toscano to see the young guitarist at the 708 Club, where the young man was performing with the Aces (Dave and Louis Myers on guitar, Fred Below on drums, and occasionally harp-blower Junior Wells). Though Toscano was unimpressed at first, the strong-willed and musically astute Dixon eventually convinced him of Rush's potential and secured a contract.

"I Can't Quit You Baby," Rush's first release with Cobra Records and a top-ten R&B hit in 1956, was recorded in Chicago with Wayne Bennett

Otis Rush hit the charts (R&B top ten) head-on with "I Can't Quit You Baby," recorded at the recommendation of Willie Dixon for Eli Toscano's Cobra label at the Kimball Hall Studio in the summer of 1956.

The West Side

Born and raised in Chicago and weaned on the blues, Michael Bloomfield (1942-1981) has been hailed as one of the most influential guitarists in pop music as well as the United States' answer to Eric Clapton.

(guitar), "Big" Walter Horton (harp), Red Holloway (tenor sax), Willie Dixon (bass), Lafayette Leake (piano), and Al Duncan (drums). An important development that arose within Rush's own band was the electrification of the bass. Second guitar player Willie D. Warren, originally from Greenwood, Mississippi, is generally credited as the first electric bass player because of his innovative style of playing only the lower strings of his guitar. Soon afterward the first Fender bass guitars appeared on the market, and it seemed like every band had to have one.

After Cobra's demise in 1959, Rush was taken to Chess only to be lost in the shuffle behind the already established names on the label. A contract with Duke Records followed in 1963, but yielded only one single and fueled Rush's growing distrust of the recording industry. Following a six-year hiatus, he recorded his first album, *Mourning in the Morning*, early in 1969. Produced by Mike Bloomfield and Nick Gravenites for Atlantic subsidiary Cotillion Records, it was recorded at one of the centers for soul in the sixties, Fame Studios in Muscle Shoals, Alabama. The album included Aaron Varnell and Joe Arnold (tenor saxes), Ronald Eades (baritone sax), Gene "Bowlegs" Miller (trumpet), Jimmy Johnson and Duane Allman (guitars), Jerry Jemmott (bass), Barry Beckett and Mark Naftalin (keyboards), and Roger Hawkins (drums).

Despite the best of intentions, however, Bloomfield and Gravenites in their eagerness and admiration ended up overproducing the album and it subsequently flopped commercially. The follow-up, *Right Place, Wrong Time*, recorded for Capitol Records in 1971 and considered by many fans to be his finest work, was inexplicably shelved until Bullfrog Records bought the rights and released it in 1976.

Underrecorded and underappreciated, the guitar innovator recognized for his ability to make the strings "sing" came out of semiretirement to record the well-received and aptly titled *Ain't Enough Comin' In* for Mercury Records in 1994.

* * * * *

Together with Otis Rush (with whom he shared a short tenure at the ill-fated Cobra), Freddie King, and Buddy Guy, Magic Sam was among the guitar innovators whose purview was the West Side of Chicago.

The West Side

Magic Sam (1937–1969)

I don't want to be Sad Sam, Poor Sam, Black Sam, Dark Sam or what have you.
—Magic Sam

Born Sam Maghett in Grenada, Mississippi, on Valentine's Day, 1937, guitarist Magic Sam (like Otis Rush) grew up listening to the records of Little Walter and Muddy Waters. When Sam was thirteen his family moved to the neighborhood of 27th Street and Calumet in Chicago, where he grew up with childhood friends Mack Thompson and Syl Johnson. Sam played his first gig at nineteen with Mack Thompson and his uncle and manager Shakey Jake's band at the 708 Club on East 47th on the West Side. Shakey Jake was born James D. Harris on April 12, 1921, in Arkansas and had made a living as a professional gambler for fifteen years before turning to music.

The set went well and gave them the confidence to make a dub of one of their numbers, "All Your Love"; then began the exhausting task of trying to generate the kind of interest that could lead to a recording contract. Eli Toscano, on the heels of his success with Otis Rush, decided to give the newcomers a chance and "All Your Love" was recorded in Chicago in 1957 with the ubiquitous Willie Dixon on bass, Mack Thompson on bass guitar, Little Brother Montgomery on piano, and Billie Stepney on drums. Shakey Jake was also given the chance to record; his release of "Call Me If You Need Me" did fairly well.

The next step was to find Sam a new name. He had been calling himself "Good Rocking Sam," but another artist was already using that name on record. Toscano suggested "Sad Sam," but that sounded dated to this new generation of bluesmen. Finally Mack Thompson derived "Magic Sam" from Maghett, and the name was firmly established by the release of his first recording for Cobra Records, "All Your Love," in 1957.

The popularity of that first release may have stilted Sam's creative growth somewhat, for he constantly returned to the same theme, with slight variations, on his subsequent releases, including "All Night Long" and "Easy Baby." In any case he was tremendously popular in Chicago until his career was interrupted by the draft in 1959. Seven months later (one in service and six in prison for desertion) he found it difficult to pick up where had he left off.

Sam recorded sporadically over the next few years for indie labels Chief, Crash, and Bright Star, culminating with the critically acclaimed *West Side Soul* album, recorded for Delmark Records in 1968. Sam's vocals came straight from the church and his blues reflected the pride that would become a defining characteristic of the soul music to emerge in the 1960s. Tragically, Magic Sam's potential would never be realized, for he succumbed to a fatal heart attack at the age of thirty-two on December 1, 1969. Sam was inducted into the Blues Foundation's Hall of Fame in 1982.

* * * * *

Eli Toscano formed his last label, Artistic, in August 1958 and moved his offices to 3346 West Roosevelt to accommodate the expansion. The first artist to join the new label was George "Buddy" Guy.

Despite a remarkable career (including the critically acclaimed album West Side Soul, *recorded for the Delmark label in 1968) that was tragically cut short by a heart attack in 1969, Magic Sam left an indelible mark on the West Side sound of Chicago blues.*

The West Side

Buddy Guy (b. 1936)

During his heyday in the 1960s, Buddy Guy...moved the blues guitar into its postmodern era.

—Robert Santelli

Born George Guy to Isabell Toliver and Sam Guy on July 30, 1936, and raised in Lettsworth, Louisiana, Buddy Guy grew up listening to Lightnin' Hopkins, John Lee Hooker, and T-Bone Walker on the radio and became part of the bridge between blues and rock and roll in the 1960s. Many white blues-rock fans compared him to Jimi Hendrix (who supposedly admitted to being influenced by Guy), and Eric Clapton has called him the greatest blues guitarist ever.

Guy's father bought him his first guitar when he was seventeen and the young man began playing professionally in and around Baton Rouge in the early 1950s. His big break came when the most popular bluesman in the area, Big Poppa (John Tilley), came to Baton Rouge without his guitar player, and Guy was chosen to fill in. He was so nervous that he blew it, but was given another chance when Poppa returned about six months later. According to author Mike Rowe, this time his friends got him so drunk that stage fright was no longer a problem. Guy joined Poppa's band and as a result had the opportunity to play with local artists like Lightnin' Slim, Lazy Lester, and Slim Harpo.

Following the advice of a friend who had gone there the year before, Guy moved to Chicago in 1957 and was eventually hired

The influence of Buddy Guy (pictured here in 1970) extended across the globe, as evidenced in the summer of 1969 when he became the first American bluesman to tour central and eastern Africa.

48

Shortly after they met at Theresa's in Chicago in 1958, Buddy Guy and Junior Wells combined to form one of the most accomplished blues bands on the West Side, touring extensively across Africa and Asia and appearing often with the Rolling Stones in Europe.

by sax player Rufus Foreman, who was a regular at Theresa's Lounge on 48th Street and Indiana Avenue. Unfortunately, Foreman lost the job before Guy even had a chance to play. After a frustrating period with no place to play, they were hired by a man named Sinclair, manager of the Big Squeeze club on the West Side. The band, including Guy, Foreman, Baby Face Willette (piano), and Hal Tidwell (drums), played there for about five months before returning to Theresa's.

In 1958 Guy, already a dynamic performer, prevailed over Otis Rush and Magic Sam in a club-sponsored "Battle of the Blues" contest, held at the Blue Flame on 55th and State streets, which led Sam to recommend him to Eli Toscano. He managed to record two singles, "Sit and Cry" and "This Is the End," for the Artistic label before it folded. More importantly, however, he had been introduced to Willie Dixon.

Toscano was known as a compulsive gambler (Rush recalled that Toscano's records made the label owner a lot of money but most of it was gambled away), and his vice may have led him to an early grave. Cobra Records and its subsidiary abruptly folded with the gangland murder of Eli Toscano, whose body was dragged from Lake Michigan in 1959. With Cobra's demise, Dixon brought Buddy Guy and Otis Rush back to Chess with him.

Guy signed with Chess Records as a session musician in 1960, playing behind such legends as Muddy Waters, Willie Dixon, Little Walter, Sonny Boy Williamson #2, and Koko Taylor. His debut under his own name was an impressive and haunting version (reminiscent of Robert Johnson) of Little Brother Montgomery's "First Time I Met the Blues," originally recorded in 1936. Guy's stage presence made him more popular than Rush (he remained with Chess as a name artist and house musician well into the 1960s), who had had only one release on the Chess label before signing with Duke Records.

Guy signed with the Vanguard label in the late 1960s and produced three outstanding albums featuring a raucous horn section: *This Is Buddy Guy, Hold That*

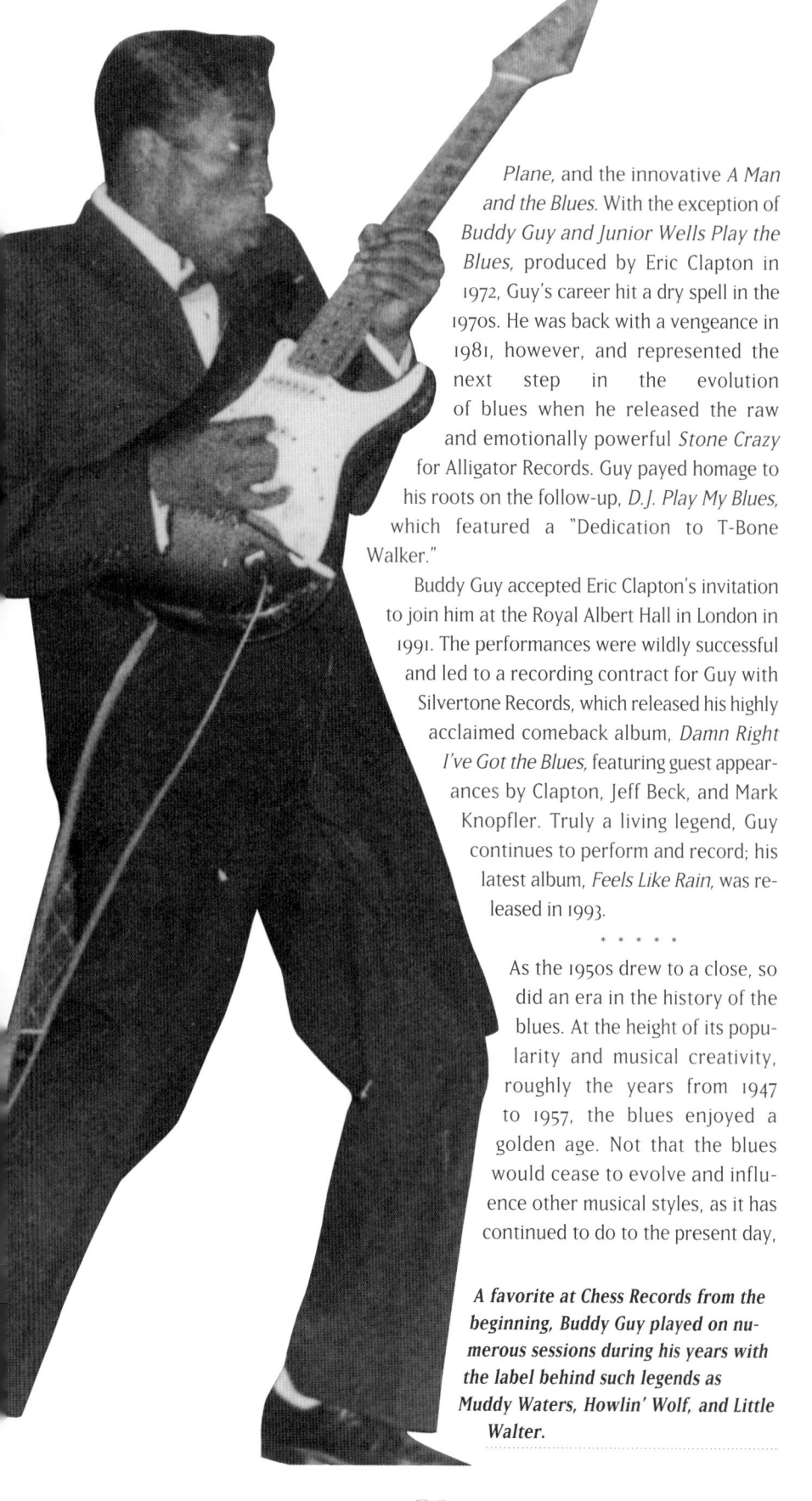

The West Side

Plane, and the innovative *A Man and the Blues*. With the exception of *Buddy Guy and Junior Wells Play the Blues*, produced by Eric Clapton in 1972, Guy's career hit a dry spell in the 1970s. He was back with a vengeance in 1981, however, and represented the next step in the evolution of blues when he released the raw and emotionally powerful *Stone Crazy* for Alligator Records. Guy payed homage to his roots on the follow-up, *D.J. Play My Blues*, which featured a "Dedication to T-Bone Walker."

Buddy Guy accepted Eric Clapton's invitation to join him at the Royal Albert Hall in London in 1991. The performances were wildly successful and led to a recording contract for Guy with Silvertone Records, which released his highly acclaimed comeback album, *Damn Right I've Got the Blues*, featuring guest appearances by Clapton, Jeff Beck, and Mark Knopfler. Truly a living legend, Guy continues to perform and record; his latest album, *Feels Like Rain*, was released in 1993.

* * * * *

As the 1950s drew to a close, so did an era in the history of the blues. At the height of its popularity and musical creativity, roughly the years from 1947 to 1957, the blues enjoyed a golden age. Not that the blues would cease to evolve and influence other musical styles, as it has continued to do to the present day,

A favorite at Chess Records from the beginning, Buddy Guy played on numerous sessions during his years with the label behind such legends as Muddy Waters, Howlin' Wolf, and Little Walter.

Described as shy and humble offstage, Buddy Guy turned into a wild showman when he got under the lights in front of an audience.

but it was during this period that the blues remained "pure" to its roots in the African American community. As we shall see, the next step in the evolution of the blues came during the British Invasion and Blues Revival of the 1960s, when white musicians began to play the blues on a large scale.

Following Len Chess' retirement from the recording business in 1965, the small Chess family of labels became huge and very commercial and began pouring out a number of mediocre albums. This continued until 1970, when Chess Records and its subsidiaries was eventually sold; Len Chess had died on October 16, 1969, and Chess Records was bought out by GRT in New York. Ralph Bass is currently racing against time to document the vast storehouse of deteriorating material at the Chess building at 321 East 21st Street. Today, Chess Records is marketed in the United States by MCA.

There were a number of independent blues labels formed in the late 1950s in Chicago, including Carl Morris Jones' C.J. label and subsidiaries Firma and Colt, Vi Muszynki's Bandera label, the Reverend H.H. Harrington's short-lived Atomic H, Al Benson's Bronzeville Records, and John Burton's El-Bee. But none of them was able to survive the onslaught of the new music of the 1960s.

Chicago blues evolved from the amplification and electrification of Delta blues, with its various strains from Texas, Louisiana, and other parts of the deep South. Traveling bluesmen from the Delta region and other parts of Mississippi who began recording careers in the 1940s and 1950s included Johnny Ace, Bobby Blue Bland, Big Boy Crudup, Big Walter Horton, Sunnyland Slim, Little Junior Parker, Otis Spann, Hound Dog Taylor, Junior Wells, and Jimmy Reed, among many others. Son Seals (b. 1942), belonging to a younger generation, was perhaps the last of the Delta bluesmen to arrive in Chicago, in 1971.

Jimmy Reed (1924–1976)

Jimmy Reed helped establish VeeJay as a competitor in the R&B recording field when he joined the roster of the fledgling record company in 1955, recording steadily with the label until it folded in 1966.

Born a sharecropper's son on September 6, 1925, in Dunleith or Leland, Mississippi, Mathias James Reed was the youngest of the ten children of Joseph and Virginia Reed. Joseph Reed was a harp player and inspired the young Jimmy to play the blues, and by the time he was seven he could pick out a few notes on the guitar. It was also around this time that he befriended Eddie Taylor, who was also picking his way along on the guitar. Although it wasn't until nearly twenty years later that they reunited, Eddie Taylor was a great influence on Jimmy Reed.

Jimmy Reed brought traditional Delta "sweet" blues with him when he moved to Chicago in 1943, but was drafted shortly after his arrival and served in the navy until the end of World War II. Reed returned to Chicago briefly following his discharge before moving to Gary, Indiana. He teamed up with Taylor again in 1949 and finally resettled in Chicago in 1953, where shortly thereafter the two men participated in a recording session with Chance Records.

After a failed audition with Chess Records, Reed and Taylor turned to VeeJay, notably the first black-owned and -managed record label, which signed them in 1955. During a time when the blues were used heavily for dancing, Jimmy Reed had five consecutive hits in 1956, outdistancing every other bluesman at the time—at least in terms of commercial success.

Reed owed much of his success to Taylor and to wife Mary Lee "Mama" Reed, who wrote many of his songs. Taylor taught Reed the rudiments of guitar and helped shape his laid-back "sweet" blues sound, which often crossed easily onto the pop charts (as did "Honest I Do" and "Baby What You Want Me to Do") and enabled him to sell more blues records in the 1950s and 1960s than any other bluesman save B.B. King.

During the 1960s, Jimmy Reed appeared at Carnegie Hall and the Apollo Theater and toured England extensively, his popularity there due at least in part to well-known covers of his songs by the Rolling Stones. He continued to tour in the 1970s, until alcoholism took its toll; Reed died in Oakland, California, on August 29, 1976. He was inducted into the Blues Foundation's Hall of Fame in 1980 and the Rock and Roll Hall of Fame in 1991.

Standin' at the Crossroads

Black musicians used the Celtic ballad (the versification AAB of the blues comes directly from it); white musicians used the black blues.
—Gerard Herzhaft

In 1949 *Billboard* replaced the "Race Music" category with "Rhythm & Blues" on the national charts. With the birth of rhythm and blues and rock and roll in the mid-1950s came the temporary death of the blues (it was reincarnated during the revival of the 1960s), a form of patricide committed by a public hungry for a new sound, which the major labels were eager to provide. The decade would be one of major upheaval in the music industry, especially with the emergence of rock and roll, which would leave many formally established musicians floundering for stable ground along with newer artists who were unsure of where to begin. In the words of bluesman Floyd Jones (1917–1990), "The beat has changed."

The first "official" rock and roll record was "Sh-Boom," by the Chords, released in 1954. White cover band the Crewcuts followed it up with a version of their own, which faired much better on the national charts (and therefore commercially) than did its black counterpart, an occurrence that became commonplace for the rest of the decade.

It was also in 1954 that Eddie Lee "Guitar Slim" Jones' (1926–1959) million-seller "The Things I Used to Do" topped *Billboard*'s R&B charts. Backed by bassist Lloyd Lambert's orchestra in 1953, Slim performed regularly at the Dew

The Crewcuts were among the first of a long line of white cover bands that made their name recording African American music when their 1954 version of "Sh-Boom" outsold the Chords' original.

Eddie "Guitar Slim" Jones held the number one position on the R&B charts for six weeks in 1954 with "The Things I Used to Do," a raw blend of gospel intensity and distorted electric guitar.

Drop Inn in New Orleans, and the group became one of the Crescent City's most popular blues bands. Slim was spotted at the club by Specialty Records talent scout Johnny Vincent, who secured a contract for the blues guitarist with Atlantic Records. With Ray Charles (b. 1930) joining Lambert's band for the session, "The Things I Used to Do" was cut on October 27, 1953. Like Magic Sam, had he lived longer (heavy drinking took its toll on February 7, 1959), Guitar Slim's "secular spirituality" would surely have become part of the bridge from blues to soul as the work of Sam Cooke (1935–1964) was the bridge from gospel to soul.

Charles Edward Berry (b. 1926) won *Billboard*'s Triple Award when "Maybelline" entered the charts and went straight to number one in August of 1955. Originally titled "Ida Red," it was recut at the Chess studios and a dub was sent to disc jockey Alan Freed at station WINS in New York. Bo Diddley (b. 1928) was already in the top ten at the time with a song of the same name.

There was a new beat on the horizon, and even veteran bluesman Muddy Waters tried to cash in on the phenomenon with releases like "She's Nineteen Years Old," with its teenage themes of girls and fast cars. Len Chess, ever cognizant of tidal changes in recording industry waters, hired A&R man Ralph Bass from the King/Federal label to keep up with current trends.

Rock and roll was firmly established by the 1960s, cutting a wide swath over the airwaves and rolling over nearly every other musical format in its path. The 1960s reduction in blues programming on the black stations was probably at first due to financial considerations, but it's fairly certain that the policy was enforced by a militant black establishment, which in the burgeoning era of Black Pride viewed with distaste anything with roots traceable to a past best forgotten.

Although bluespeople had always seen the recording business as secondary to public performances, airplay was an essential part of these performers' financial success. Records provided publicity; a hit record could ensure steady work in the clubs or on the road, and any royalties could then be considered the icing on the cake. So the change in policy of the radio stations meant a serious loss of earning power.

Then in 1961, Peter "Memphis Slim" Chatman (1915–1988) and Willie Dixon organized the American Folk Blues Festival, which began the first of many European tours in 1962. As a result, the Rolling Stones (who took their name from a Muddy Waters song) and other British bands began recording a number of blues standards, thereby helping to launch the blues revival of the 1960s, which continued well into the 1980s.

In the United States, a growing interest in American folk music formed on college campuses in the northeast and soon spread to the rest of the country. Focusing first on traditional American folk songs, interest soon blossomed in the direction of bluegrass, ragtime, acoustic country blues, and, in a roundabout way from across the seas, electric blues.

A great blues and boogie-woogie piano player and composer of the blues standard "Everyday I Have the Blues," Memphis Slim was largely ignored by the American public for much of his career, leading to his self-exile in Paris, France, beginning in 1962.

American Folk Blues Festival

John Mayall, leader of the influential blues-rock band the Bluesbreakers, which he formed in London in 1964, is pictured here at the 1969 Newport Jazz Festival in New York City, shortly after recording his last album in the U.K., Looking Back.

Prior to the British Invasion set in motion by the Beatles and Rolling Stones in 1964, there was an American "invasion" of European shores in the 1950s. Big Bill Broonzy was the first to bring American blues to Europe and exerted a huge influence on the developing British rock bands during his many return visits following the first in 1951. An ailing Broonzy later passed the torch to Muddy Waters, who began touring overseas in 1958.

Produced by Horst Lippmann and Fritz Rau, two German jazz enthusiasts who realized that European audiences were largely unfamiliar with the blues except as a source from which jazz evolved, the first American Folk Blues Festival toured Western Europe in 1962 featuring performances by Willie Dixon, Memphis Slim, John Lee Hooker, Sonny Terry, Brownie McGhee, Shakey Jake, T-Bone Walker, and Helen Humes. The phenomenal success of the 1962 tour inspired Lippman and Rau to make the festival an annual event, which is exactly what it became for the next ten years.

Although the performances were very well received and met with critical acclaim, the European audience reaction at first perplexed American bluespeople. It seems that European audiences showed their appreciation of blues the same as they would classical music, with quiet respect and polite applause. But, as Bruce Iglauer has remarked, "When blues works right, there isn't a line between the performer and the audience...it's almost like being in church." It took some time for the artists to accustom themselves to the lack of audience participation.

The format of the festival itself had its share of shortcomings, most notably the shortage of performance time allotted each artist (due in part to the overbooking of the events). The last festival, in 1972, was poorly received, largely due to the proliferation of competing events that were better organized and aimed at a more sophisticated and knowledgeable blues audience.

However, the historical significance of the events remain, instrumental as they were in introducing the blues to a new audience overseas, many of whom witnessed for the first time the music of Sonny Boy Williamson, Muddy Waters, Otis Spann, Lonnie Johnson, Big Joe Williams, M.T. Murphy, Victoria Spivey, J.B. Lenoir, and many others at the annual event. In return, American audiences were reintroduced to the blues, which had existed in their own backyards for years, thanks to the British rockers' appreciation of the indigenous music of the United States.

The British Invasion

The first white blues performers were proud to play with the masters of the art, and blacks were just as proud to have them at their side. It was a double-barrelled vindication: black culture was being accepted by whites and whites were being allowed to participate in it...the blues had become a mulatto.

—Julio Finn

In the late 1950s, Great Britain experienced a blues explosion in the form of the "skiffle" craze (based in traditional American blues, many British skiffle bands went so far as to attempt to recreate the homemade guitars or "diddley bows" that so many Delta bluesmen grew up with). Led by guitarist Alexis Korner (1928–1984) and harp player Cyril Davies (1932–1964), Blues Incorporated proved to be the band from which nearly every major British musician would draw influence, including John Mayall (b. 1934), Eric Clapton, the Rolling Stones, the

Hound Dog Taylor purchased his first electric guitar in 1957 and recorded for the first time that same year. His first album, however, was not released until 1971, a year after he had performed to an enthusiastic audience at the Ann Arbor Blues Festival with his band the House Rockers.

The British Invasion

Beatles, Led Zeppelin, Jeff Beck, Peter Green, and Eric Burdon (b. 1941), to name a few. Formed in London in 1961 with drummer Charlie Watts (b. 1941) an original member, Blues Incorporated performed weekly at the Marquee Club and was often fronted by Mick Jagger (b. 1943).

By the time the Rolling Stones (firmly rooted in the blues of Waters and Dixon) followed the Beatles (who took their cue from Elvis Presley and Buddy Holly) to American shores in 1964, the barriers within the recording industry were rapidly breaking down, in effect mirroring the battering of anachronistic social conventions during the Civil Rights Movement.

As John Mayall, founder of the seminal British blues band the Bluesbreakers, recalled for *Guitar Player* magazine, "John Lee Hooker was the first real blues guitar player we backed up. This was in 1965. It was a very humbling experience, because we all thought we were shit-hot players and knew what it was all about. Then you get Hooker onstage and what you know flies out the window."

The American blues-rock fusion of guitarist Mike Bloomfield (1942–1981), the Paul Butterfield (1942–1987) Band, harpist Charlie Musselwhite (b. 1944), the Blues Project, guitarist Elvin Bishop (b. 1942), and, later, guitar legends Johnny Winter (b. 1944) and the late Stevie Ray Vaughan developed largely in response to the British blues-rock influence of bands like Savoy Brown, the Yardbirds, the Faces, and the original Fleetwood Mac.

Naturally, recording companies renewed their lagging interest in the blues in response to public demand, as Son House experienced in April 1965, when he returned to the recording studio following a thirty-five-year absence. Instead of the limited production equipment of a Library of Congress field recording, however, House would benefit from the excellent sound technology and distribution capa-

Robert Cray has taken the blues to the next stage with the tremendous success he has enjoyed since 1985. Inspired by a performance by Albert Collins at the University of Tacoma, Washington, the modern bluesman holds the record for W.C. Handy awards.

The British Invasion

bilities of a major record company: Columbia. Much credit for the success of the resulting album, *Father of Folk Blues,* is due to Al Wilson (1943–1970), future lead vocalist of the American blues band Canned Heat.

Bob Koester of the independent Delmark Records in Chicago was also instrumental in reviving the careers of forgotten blues musicians. In 1962 he signed Sleepy John Estes (1904–1977) to his label after filmmaker David Blumenthal found the bluesman alive and well in the course of his research for the documentary *Citizen South—Citizen North.*

Beginning in the 1970s and continuing to the present day, blues enthusiasts like Bruce Iglauer (b. 1947) of Alligator Records in Chicago have been keeping the blues alive. Actually, Iglauer worked for Delmark before starting his own label upon Koester's refusal to sign Hound Dog Taylor (1917–1975) in 1970. In the two decades since the label's inception, Alligator artists have earned the distinction of over two dozen Grammy awards and close to fifty W.C. Handy awards. On the frontlines of contemporary blues, Alligator's roster has included Koko Taylor (b. 1935), who made Willie Dixon's "Wang Dang Doodle" a million-seller in 1966; barrelhouse-style piano-player Katie Webster (b. 1939); Zydeco King Clifton Chenier (b. 1925); Expressway Lounge regular Son Seals; slide-guitarist J.B. Hutto's (1925–1983) nephew and second-generation bluesman "Lil' Ed" Williams (b. 1955) and the Blues Imperials; the guitar prowess of the father and son team of Lonnie (b. 1933) and Ronnie Brooks; the funk/blues of the Kinsey Report; "Smoking Gun" Robert Cray (b. 1953); and Texas string-bender Johnny Copeland (b. 1937).

Lacking the space necessary for an in-depth study of the development of contemporary blues, we can turn to the well-versed John Mayall, again from an interview with *Guitar Player*: "It's something blues players have done since the beginning. They know there's never anything original, and they know what it is about a song that creates magic. They bring their individuality to it, put their stamp on it, and create something completely new."

A native of Louisiana, where he was an avid fan of the country music radio show Louisiana Hayride, *Johnny "Clyde" Copeland learned to play guitar in the black clubs of Houston, Texas, where he moved in 1950. He was soon accomplished enough to play with the likes of T-Bone Walker, Bobby "Blue" Bland, and Big Mama Thornton; he even toured with Otis Redding and Eddie Floyd.*

Epilogue

Through all of the sorrow of the Sorrow Songs there breathes a hope—a faith in the ultimate justice of things....Sometime, somewhere, men will judge men by their souls and not by their skins.
—William E.B. Dubois, *The Souls of Black Folk*

The blues are part of the American heritage of citizens whose ancestors suffered what has been described as a "peculiar" fate. Born in a time of severe racial oppression, the blues gave hope to the disenfranchised African American when precious little hope was to be found. Through the bitter days of Reconstruction, the ravages of natural catastrophe, and two world wars, and under the awesome burden of racism and ignorance, the blues persevered. They danced, shouted, cried; the bluespeople spoke through, to, and for their brothers and sisters, and through the blues they survived. The fact that more than four hundred years of slavery could not eradicate the African spirit is a testament to the strength of the spirit itself.

In 1980 the newly organized Blues Foundation inaugurated the W.C. Handy Blues Awards, with ceremonies on Beale Street in Memphis on November 16. The polling process selected fifty-nine winners, including twenty inductees into the Blues Hall of Fame. Among the winners were Albert Collins, Koko Taylor, Jimmy Johnson (b. 1928),

Pictured here at the fourth American Folk Blues Festival, Fairfield Halls, England, in October 1965 are (foreground, left to right) Big Mama Thornton, Big Walter Horton, and J.B. Lenoir.

Epilogue

Albert Collins continued to electrify audiences well into the 1980s, earning a Grammy, several W.C. Handy awards, and making several appearances on television. His commercial success culminated in 1986 with a triumphant appearance at Live-Aid.

Professor Longhair (1918–1980), Esther Phillips (1935–1984), and Willie Mae "Big Mama" Thornton (1926–1984). As presented in *Living Blues* magazine (at this writing celebrating its twenty-fifth anniversary), among the winners of the 1995 W.C. Handy Blues Awards in various categories are Buddy Guy, the Charlie Musselwhite Band, Otis Rush, Etta James, Charles Brown, Pinetop Perkins, Katie Webster, Koko Taylor, Gatemouth Brown, Solomon Burke, Jimmy Rogers, and Eric Clapton, among others.

Whether you call it soul/blues, "deep" blues, rhythm and blues, or by any other name, the blues is alive and well in the 1990s. In 1995, for instance, Antone's Nightclub in Austin, Texas, celebrated its twentieth anniversary; the Sunflower River Blues & Gospel Festival enjoyed its eighth year in Clarksdale; the twenty-third annual San Francisco Blues Festival, with a tribute to living blues legend John Lee Hooker, took place; the eighth annual Bull Durham Blues Festival in North Carolina welcomed George Thorogood's Fabulous Thunderbirds and Bobby "Blue" Bland; and the Atlanta Heritage Blues Festival held a tribute to guitar legend Lowell Fulson.

Times have surely changed, and the torch is being passed to the next generation of bluespeople even while the elders of the form look on. Lynn White (b. 1953) shared her thoughts on today's blues for *Living Blues* magazine: "I want to carry people into a new dimension of blues....Black or white, Chinese, or whatever, they can relate to it, and so I felt like that's what I've been doin', you know. It's still carryin' the same message. It just has a different beat to it...."

However the beat may change, blues remains an essential base for much of contemporary popular music today, and a timeless element of the world's musical heritage. As jazz guitar legend and elder statesman Kenny Burrell (b. 1931) reflected so eloquently in the liner notes to his 1968 release for the Verve label, *Blues—The Common Ground*: "The blues is T-Bone Walker, Jimmy Reed, The Staples Singers, John Coltrane, sometimes the Beatles and Rolling Stones or the Buffalo Springfield, and many others. One can detect a blues flavor in a flamenco tune, a Gypsy folk song, in the folk music of most cultures, because the blues reflects the emotions of the common man. It is part of one powerful force with many channels, and that force is the soul of man."

Suggested Reading

Suggested Reading

Bebey, Francis. *African Music: A People's Art*. New York: Lawrence Hill, 1975.

Bird, Christiane. *The Jazz and Blues Lover's Guide to the U.S*. New York: Addison-Wesley, 1994.

Brunning, Bob. *Blues: The British Connection*. United Kingdom: Blandford Press, 1986.

Dixon, Willie, and Don Snowden. *I Am the Blues: The Willie Dixon Story*. London: Quartet Books, 1989.

Ferris, William. *Blues from the Delta*. New York: Anchor Press, 1978.

Finn, Julio. *The Bluesman: The Musical Heritage of Black Men and Women in the Americas*. New York: Interlink Books, 1992.

Haskins, James. *Black Music in America: A History Through Its People*. New York: HarperCollins Publishers, 1987.

Herzhaft, Gerard. *Encyclopedia of the Blues*. Fayetteville, Ark.: University of Arkansas Press, 1992.

Oliver, Paul, ed. *The Blackwell Guide to Recorded Blues*. Cambridge, England: Blackwell Publishers, 1994.

Oliver, Paul. *Blues Fell This Morning: Meaning in the Blues*. 2nd ed. Cambridge, England: Cambridge University Press, 1990.

Oliver, Paul. *Blues Off the Record: Thirty Years of Blues Commentary*. New York: Da Capo Press, 1984.

Rowe, Mike. *Chicago Blues: The City & the Music*. New York: Da Capo Press, 1975.

Rubin, Dave. *Inside the Blues, 1942–1982: Four Decades of the Greatest Electric Blues Guitarists*. Milwaukee: Hal Leonard, 1995.

Santelli, Robert. *The Big Book of the Blues*. New York: Penguin Books, 1993.

Shaw, Arnold. *Honkers and Shouters: The Golden Years of Rhythm & Blues*. New York: Macmillan Publishing Company, 1978.

Sonnier, Austin, Jr. *A Guide to the Blues: History, Who's Who, Research Sources*. Westport, Conn.: Greenwood Press, 1994.

Southern, Eileen. *The Music of Black Americans: A History*. New York: W.W. Norton & Company, 1983.

Vance, Rubert B. *Human Factors in Cotton Culture*. Chapel Hill, N.C.: University of North Carolina Press, 1929.

Suggested Listening

Bland, Bobby. *Two Steps from the Blues* (MCA)
Bloomfield, Michael. *The Best of Michael Bloomfield* (Takoma)
Brooks, Lonnie. *Bayou Lightning* (Alligator)
Brown, Charles. *Drifting Blues* (Pathe/Marconi)
Brown, Clarence "Gatemouth." *Texas Swing* (Rounder)
Butterfield, Paul. *The Paul Butterfield Blues Band* (Elektra)
Collins, Albert. *Ice Pickin'* (Alligator)
Cray, Robert. *Bad Influence* (Hightone)
Dixon, Willie. *The Willie Dixon Chess Box* (Chess)
Fulson, Lowell. *Reconsider Baby* (Chess)
Guy, Buddy. *A Man and the Blues* (Vanguard)
Hooker, John Lee. *Boogie Chillen* (Charly)
Hound Dog Taylor. *Beware of the Dog* (Alligator)
Howlin' Wolf. *Moanin' in the Moonlight* (Chess)
James, Elmore. *Shake Your Moneymaker* (Charly)
King, Albert. *Born Under a Bad Sign* (Stax)
King, B.B. *Live and Well* (ABC)
King, Freddie. *Let's Hideaway and Dance Away* (King/Federal)
Lightnin' Hopkins. *How Many More Years I Got* (Fantasy)
Magic Sam. *Easy Baby* (Charly)
Nighthawk, Robert. *Bricks in My Pillow* (Pearl)
Robinson, Fenton. *Special Road* (Black Magic)
Rush, Otis. *Mourning in the Morning* (Cotillion)
Seals, Son. *Bad Axe* (Alligator)
Shines, Johnny. *Standing at the Crossroads* (Testament)
Taylor, Koko. *The Earthshaker* (Alligator)
Various artists. *Blues at Newport* (Vanguard)
Various artists. *The Blues Came Down from Memphis* (Charly)
Various artists. *Chicago Blues* (Chess)
Vaughan, Stevie Ray. *Texas Flood* (Epic)
Waters, Muddy. *The Muddy Waters Chess Box* (Chess)
Wells, Junior. *Hoodoo Man Blues* (Delmark)
Winter, Johnny. *Guitar Slinger* (Alligator)
Young, Mighty Joe. *Legacy of the Blues* (Sonet)

Photography Credits

Cover: Albert Collins: ©Michael Putland/Retna Ltd.; Albert King: ©David Redfern/Redferns/Retna Ltd.; neon sign: ©Dennis Mac Donald/Envision; Chicago skyline: ©Michael J. Howell/Envision; guitar (left): ©Tony Mottram/Retna Ltd.; telecaster (right): ©James Kozrya

Interior
©Archive Photos: Frank Driggs Collection: pp. 12, 18, 27, 52, 53, 55; Tucker Ranson: p. 48
©Ray Avery's Jazz Archives: pp. 2, 31, 44
©Delta Images/Leslie R. Chin: p. 61
©Frank Driggs Collection: pp. 21, 25, 47
©Envision: Jean Higgins: p. 23; B.W. Hoffmann: p. 34; Dennis Mac Donald: p. 30
©Globe Photos, Inc.: Robert Fitzgerald: p. 56; Walter Iooss, Jr.: p. 51
©James Kozara: p. 11 bottom
©North Wind Picture Archives: pp. 8, 9
©Redferns/Retna, Ltd.: pp. 35, 43, 50; James Barron: p. 60; Berard: p. 59; Peter Figen: p. 41; Max Jones Files: p. 57; Tim Hall: p. 49; Michael Putland: p. 22; David Redfern: pp. 11 top, 20, 28, 29, 32, 36–37, 38, 39, 42, 45; Susan Rutman: p. 58
©Scala/Art Resource: p. 6
©Photo Courtesy of Showtime Archives, Toronto: pp. 14, 15, 16; Rick Coleman: p. 54; Colin Escott: p. 26; Ivey Gladin: p. 13
©Stock Montage: p. 7
©UPI/Bettmann: p. 10

Index

Ace, Johnny, 28, 51
Ain't Enough Comin' In, 45
Alexander, Alger "Texas," 19
"All Night Long," 26, 46
"All Your Love," 46
American Folk Blues Festival, 55, 56
Ammons, Gene, 40

"**B**aby What You Want Me to Do," 52
Backwater blues, 9–17
"Battle of the Blues," 21
Beck, Jeff, 28, 50, 58
Below, Fred, 26, 40, 44
Bennett, Wayne, 32, 44
Berry, Chuck, 42, 54
Big Crawford, 36, 40
Bishop, Elvin, 58
Bland, Bobby "Blue," 28, 32, 51, 56, 59, 61
Bloomfield, Mike, 45, *45*, 58
Blue Flames, 24
Bluegrass, 55
Bluesbreakers, 32, 56, 58
Blues Foundation Hall of Fame, 21, 26, 29, 30, 40, 42, 46, 52, 60
Blues Imperials, 59
Blues Incorporated, 57, 58
Blues Project, 58
"Boogie Chillen," 31, 32
Booker T. & the MG's, 29
Broonzy, Big Bill, 34, 36, 38
Brown, Charles, 61
Brown, Clarence "Gatemouth," 19, 22, 61
Brown, Piney, 22
Brown, Shelby, 9
Burton, John, 20
Burton, Larry, 22

"**C**all It Stormy Monday," 19
"Call Me If You Need Me," 46
Caston, Leonard "Baby Doo," 42
Charles, Ray, 54
Chatman, Peter "Memphis Slim," 40, 55, *55*, 56
Chenier, Clifton, 59
Chicago blues, 32, 33–42
Christian, Charlie, 11, 19, 28
Clapton, Eric, 19, 28, 48, 50, 57, 61
Clay, Francis, 39, 40
Collins, Albert, 19, 22, *22*, 60
"Collins' Shuffle," 22
"Coming Home," 17
Cooke, Sam, 54
Copeland, Johnny, 59, *59*
Country blues, 13, 21, 55
"Country Blues," 35
Cray, Robert, 32, 58, *58*, 59
"Crazy Blues," 12
Crewcuts, 53, *53*

Crudup, Arthur "Big Boy," 2, *2*, 16, 32, 36, 51
Curtis, James "Peck," 13, *13*, 36

"**D**avies, Cyril, 57
Davis, Maxwell, 17
Dawkins, Jimmy, 43
"DeFrost," 22
Delta blues, 15, 18, 21, 32, 33, 35, 36, 38, 40, 51, 52, 88
"Destruction," 24
Diddley, Bo, 54
Dixon, Willie, 26, 32, 40, 41–42, *41*, *42*, 43, 44, 45, 46, 49, 55, 56, 58, 59
Durham, Eddie, 11, 19
"Dust My Broom," 14, 15, 16

"**E**asy Baby," 46
Eckstine, Billy, 40
Edwards, David "Honeyboy," 13
Evans, Elgin, 38, 40
"Everyday I Have the Blues," 30, 55
Every Hour Blues Boys, 20

"**F**eel Like Going Home," 36
Ferris, William, 9
Field hollers, 8
"First Time I Met the Blues," 49
Fitzgerald, Ella, 40
"Fly Right Little Girl," 36
Folk music, 55
Foreman, Rufus, 49
Foster, "Baby Face" Leroy, 38
Four Jumps of Jive, 42
Freed, Alan, 40, 54
Freeman, Sonny, 30
"The Freeze," 22
"Frosty," 22
Fulson, Lowell, 19, 21, 30, 32, 61

Glenn, Lloyd, 19, 30
"Goodbye Baby," 17
Gospel music, 13, 29, 30, 33, 88
"The Gospel Train," 8
"Got My Mojo Working," 40
Green, Peter, 58
Griots, 7
Groove Boys, 29
"Guitar Blues," 11
"Guitar Rag," 11
Guitar Slim, 19
Guy, George "Buddy," 19, 42, 45, 46, 48–50, *48*, *49*, *50*, *51*, 60, *60*, 61
"Gypsy Woman," 36

Handy, W.C., 12, 23
"Hard Day Blues," 36
Hare, Pat, 24, 37, 39, 40
Harmony Kings, 29
Harris, Wynonie, 21
"Hawaiian Boogie," 17
Hawkins, Roger, 45
Hendrix, Jimi, 11, 19, 29, 48
"Hide Away," 20
Hill, Big Bill, 17
Hite, Les, 19, 21, *21*

Hokum Boys, 34
Holly, Buddy, 58
"Honest I Do," 52
"Hoochie Coochie Man," 38, 40
Hooker, Earl, 32, 40
Hooker, John Lee, 19, 30–32, *31*, *32*, 48, 56, 58
Hopkins, Lightnin', 19, 22, 48
Horton, Big Walter, 32, 39, 45, 51, 60, *60*
Hosten, Robert Earl, 15
House, Eddie James "Son," 35, 58
Howlin' Wolf, 23–26, *25*, *26*, 36, 37, 42, 50
"How Many More Years," 25
Humes, Helen, 56
Hymns and Spiritual Songs (Watts), 8

"**I** Believe," 17
"I Be's Troubled," 35
"I Can't Be Satisfied," 36
"I Can't Quit You Baby," 43, 44
"I Got a Break Baby," 19
"I Just Want to Make Love to You," 40
"I Love My Baby," 26
"It Hurts Me Too," 17

Jackson, Al, 29
Jackson, Jump, 40
Jacobs, "Little" Walter, 13, 36, 38, 40, 42, 44, 46, 49, 50
Jagger, Mick, 58
James, Elmore, 13, *14*, 14–17, *16*
James, Etta, 61
James, "Homesick," 17
Jefferson, Blind Lemon, 18, 19, 29, 31
Jemmott, Jerry, 45
Jethro, Duke, 30
Jim Crow laws, 9, 10
Johnson, Jimmy, 45, 60
Johnson, Lonnie, 11, 18, 21, 28, 56
Johnson, Robert, 11, 13, 14, 15, 24, 35, 49
Johnson, Syl, 46
Johnson, Willie, 24, 26
"Johnson Machine Gun," 36
Jones, Casey, 22
Jones, Eddie Lee "Guitar Slim," 53, *54*
Jones, Floyd, 53
Jones, Johnnie, 17
Jordan, Louis, 19, 20, 22, 36

Kansas City Red, 16
King, Albert, 17, 19, 20, 28, 29, *29*, 44
King, B.B., 11, 20, 21, 22, 25, 26, 27–28, *27*, *28*, 29, 30, 32, 44, 52
King, Freddie, 17, 19, 20, *20*, 45
King Biscuit Time, 13, 23, 28
Knopfler, Mark, 50
Korner, Alexis, 57

Lambert, Lloyd, 53
Lang, Eddie, 21

Index

"Last Night," 29
Lauchie, Leo, 30
"Laundromat Blues," 29
Lazy Lester, 48
Leadbelly, 19
Leake, Lafayette, 45
Led Zeppelin, 58
Lenoir, J.B., 56, 60, *60*
Lightnin' Slim, 48
"Little Anna Mae," 36
Littlejohn, Johnny, 37
Lobos, 32
Lockwood, Robert "Junior," 13, 15, 16, 20, 28, 36
Lomax, Alan, 35
London, Mel, 17
"Long Distance Call," 40
Love, Willie, 13, *13*
Ludella, 37
Lunceford, Jimmie, 22

Magic Sam, 46, *47*, 49, 54
"Make a Little Love," 17
"Mama Don't Allow Me to Stay Out All Night Long," 31
"Mannish Boy," 40
Mayall, John, 29, 32, 56, *56*, 57, 58
McGhee, Brownie, 56
McMurphy, Lillian, 16
"Mean Old Frisco," 2
"Mean Old World," 19
Memphis blues, 23–33
"Memphis Blues," 12, 23
Memphis Minnie, 36
Memphis Slim, 40, 55, *55*, 56
Miller, Rice. *See* Williamson, Sonny Boy #2.
Minstrels, 10
Mississippi blues, 21
Mitchell, Odell, 29
"Moanin' At Midnight," 25
Montgomery, Little Brother, 46, 49
Moonglows, 42
Moore, Tutney, 15
Morganfield, McKinley. *See* Waters, Muddy.
Morton, Jelly Roll, 34
Mourning in the Morning, 45
Musselwhite, Charlie, 32, 58, 61
Myers, Louis, 43, 44

Nighthawk, Robert, 13, 32, 36, 42
"No Place to Go," 26

O'Dell, Frock, 15
Oliver, King, 34

Parker, Little Junior, 51
Patton, Charley, 24, 31, 35
Perkins, Pinetop, 37, 40, 61
Phillips, Earl, *26*
Phillips, Esther, 61
Presley, Elvis, 2, 58

Race records, 12, 28, 53
Rainey, Gertrude "Ma," 10
Redding, Otis, 59

Reed, Jimmy, 29, 32, 51, 52, *52*, 61
Reed, Mary Lee "Mama," 52
Right Place, Wrong Time, 45
Robinson, Bobby, 17
Robinson, Jimmy Lee, 20
Rock and roll, 55
Rock and Roll Hall of Fame, 21, 26, 30, 32, 40, 52
Rocking Four, 36
Rogers, Jimmy, 13, 20, 36–37, *37*, 38, 61
Rolling Stones, 32, 52, 55, 56, 57, 58, 61
"Rollin' Stone," 38
Rubin, Dave, 14
Rush, Otis, 19, 42, 43, *43*, 44, *44*, 45, 49, 61

"**S**t. Louis Blues," 12, 23
Sands, Kenny, 30
Santana, Carlos, 32
Scott, Bobby, 22
Scott, Clifford, 20
Scott, Sonny, 20
Seals, Son, 59
Shakey Jake, 46, 56
Sharecropping, 9, 15
"Sh-Boom," 53
"She Moves Me," 40
"She's Nineteen Years Old," 55
Shines, Johnny, 32
"Sit and Cry," 49
Skiffle, 57
"The Sky Is Crying," 17
Slack, Freddie, 19, 21, *21*
Slavery, 6, 6, 7, 7, 8, 9
Slim Harpo, 48
Smith, Claude, 36
Smith, Floyd, 11
Smith, "Little" George, 39
Smith, Mamie, 12, *12*
Smith, Willie, 39
"Smokestack Lightning," 15
"Smoking Gun," 59
Snow, Eddie, 29
Spann, Otis, 26, 32, 38, 39, 51, 56
Sparks, Aaron "Pinetop," 30
Spirituals, 8, 10
Spivey, Victoria, 56
"Spoonful," 26
Stackhouse, Houston, 13
Staple Singers, 61
Steele, Willie, 24, 26
Stepney, Billie, 46
Stidham, Arbee, 43
Strong, Henry, 38, 39
Sumlin, Hubert, 26, *26*, 37
Sunnyland Slim, 32, 36, 51

Taylor, Eddie, 17, 20, 32, 52
Taylor, Hound Dog, 32, 51, 57, *57*, 59
Taylor, Koko, 49, 59, 60, 61
Taylor, Robert "Dudlow," 13, *13*, 36
"Teaching the Blues," 32
Texas blues, 18–21
"That's All Right," 2, 20, 36
"The Things I Used to Do," 53, 54

"This Is the End," 49
"This Morning," 29
Thompson, Mack, 46
Thompson, Sonny, 20
Thornton, Willie Mae "Big Mama," 59, 60, *60*, 61
Thorogood, George, 32, 61
"Three O'Clock Blues," 28
"The Thrill Is Gone," 30
Tidwell, Hal, 49
Tilley, John, 48
"Trinity River Blues," 19
Tubman, Harriet, 8
Tucker, Luther, 40
Turner, Big Joe, 21
Turner, Ike, 25, 29

U2, 30
Underground Railroad, 8
Upchurch, Phil, 32
Urban blues, 21, 32, 33, 38

Varnell, Aaron, 45
Vaughan, Stevie Ray, 17, 19, 58

Walker, T-Bone, 11, *11*, 18, *18*, 19, 20, 21, *21*, 22, 28, 29, 31, 32, 48, 50, 56, 59, 61
"Walkin' Blues," 38
"Walking by Myself," 20
"Wang Dang Doodle," 59
Ware, Eddie, 36
Warren, Willie, 45
Waters, Muddy, 13, 20, 26, 32, 34, 35–36, *35*, 36, 37, 38, *38*, 39, *39*, 40, 42, 44, 46, 49, 50, 55, 56, 58
Watts, Isaac, 8, *8*
Weaver, Sylvester, 11
Webster, Katie, 59, 61
Wells, Junior, 40, 44, 49, 51
West Side blues, 43–52
West Side Soul, 46, 47
"When Love Comes to Town," 30
White, Bukka, 28
White, Precious, 15
"Wichita Falls Blues," 19
Wilkins, Joe "Willie," 13, *13*, 36
Willette, Baby Face, 49
Williams, Big Joe, 56
Williams, "Lil' Ed," 59
Williamson, Sonny Boy, 28, 34, 36, 37, 38, 56
Williamson, Sonny Boy #2, 13, *13*, 15, 16, 17, 24, 49
Willis, Bill, 20
Wilson, Al, 59
Wilson, Kim, 37
Winter, Johnny, 28, 32, 58
Witherspoon, Jimmy, 21
Woodfork, "Poor Bob," 44
Work songs, 10, 88
Wynn, Jim, 21

Young, Willow, 22

Zydeco, 59